Official Tourism Websites

TOURISM AND CULTURAL CHANGE
Series Editors: Professor Mike Robinson, *Centre for Tourism and Cultural Change, Leeds Metropolitan University, Leeds, UK* and Dr Alison Phipps, *University of Glasgow, Scotland, UK*

Understanding tourism's relationships with culture(s) and vice versa, is of ever-increasing significance in a globalising world. This series will critically examine the dynamic inter-relationships between tourism and culture(s). Theoretical explorations, research-informed analyses, and detailed historical reviews from a variety of disciplinary perspectives are invited to consider such relationships.

Full details of all the books in this series and of all our other publications can be found on http://www.channelviewpublications.com, or by writing to Channel View Publications, St Nicholas House, 31-34 High Street, Bristol BS1 2AW, UK.

TOURISM AND CULTURAL CHANGE
Series Editors: Professor Mike Robinson, *Centre for Tourism and Cultural Change, Leeds Metropolitan University, Leeds, UK* and Dr Alison Phipps, *University of Glasgow, Scotland, UK*

Official Tourism Websites
A Discourse Analysis Perspective

Richard W. Hallett and
Judith Kaplan-Weinger

CHANNEL VIEW PUBLICATIONS
Bristol • Buffalo • Toronto

Library of Congress Cataloging in Publication Data
A catalog record for this book is available from the Library of Congress.
Hallett, Richard W.
Official Tourism Websites: A Discourse Analysis Perspective/Richard W. Hallett
and Judith Kaplan-Weinger.
Tourism and Cultural Change: 23
Includes bibliographical references and index.
1. Tourism–Computer network resources. 2. Web sites. 3. World Wide Web.
I. Kaplan-Weinger, Judith. II. Title. III. Series.
G149.7.H35 2010
025.06′91–dc22 2010005007

British Library Cataloguing in Publication Data
A catalogue entry for this book is available from the British Library.

ISBN-13: 978-1-84541-137-4 (hbk)
ISBN-13: 978-1-84541-136-7 (pbk)

Channel View Publications
UK: St Nicholas House, 31-34 High Street, Bristol BS1 2AW, UK.
USA: UTP, 2250 Military Road, Tonawanda, NY 14150, USA.
Canada: UTP, 5201 Dufferin Street, North York, Ontario M3H 5T8, Canada.

The policy of Multilingual Matters/Channel View Publications is to use papers that
are natural, renewable and recyclable products, made from wood grown in sustainable
forests. In the manufacturing process of our books, and to further support our policy,
preference is given to printers that have FSC and PEFC Chain of Custody certification.
The FSC and/or PEFC logos will appear on those books where full certification has been
granted to the printer concerned.

Typeset by Datapage International Ltd.
Printed and bound in Great Britain by Short Run Press Ltd.

Dedications

(Rick Hallett) This book is dedicated to my parents, Don and Ruth Hallett, and my wife, Jill Hallett. Without their support, my virtual and physical travels would not have been possible, much less worthwhile.

(Judith Kaplan-Weinger) My travels have been those of the heart – from my parents, Evelyn and Milton Kaplan; to my husband, Larry Weinger; to my children, Sarah, Jacob, Benjamin and Joseph. I am so proud to be your daughter, your wife, your mother. You are my world.

Contents

Acknowledgements

We are extremely grateful to a number of people for their advice and support. In addition to those scholars who listened to our formal conference presentations and lectures as well as our informal talk about the topic of the discourse of tourism and gave us feedback, we give special thanks to the following people:

- to Sarah Williams and Elinor Robertson at Channel View Publications Ltd/Multilingual Matters for their guidance and patience;
- to Nisha Rahul for her focused reading and editing;
- to both Northeastern Illinois University for Rick's sabbatical during the 2006–2007 academic year and the Centre for Tourism and Cultural Change (CTCC) at Leeds Metropolitan University, where Rick spent part of his sabbatical;
- to Mike Robinson at the CTCC, without whose guidance and support this book would never have come to fruition;
- to Phil Long at the CTCC for his recommended readings and sage advice;
- to our colleagues in the Department of Linguistics at Northeastern Illinois University, Shahrzad Mahootian and John Boyle, for their ears and hearts;
- to our graduate students in linguistics at Northeastern Illinois University for their interest, input and inspiration (in particular, Paul Bick, Hannaliisa Savolainen, Laila Hualpa, Inge Stockburger, Marco Shappeck, Robin Hunt, Sarah Russe, Kathy Howell and Barbara Vaughan);
- to Jill Hallett for being one of the best proofreaders we have ever known.

We'd also like to thank the following organisations for giving us permissions to use various images and material throughout the book:

Burma Campaign UK
Estonian Tourist Board
Gary South Shore Railcats
Harris Law Firm, P.C. (Gary Steelheads)

James Lane (Gary Centennial)
Lithuanian State Department of Tourism
Louisiana Department of Culture, Recreation and Tourism
National Baseball Hall of Fame
New Orleans Tourism Marketing Corporation
Turismo de Santiago
Working Dog (Jetlag Travel Series)

Foreword

For as long as anyone can remember, I have been afflicted by wanderlust. I first became aware of my condition as a child sitting with my parents in church one Sunday morning. At one point during the service, the minister announced that the youth group was planning a trip to Brazil. Excited about the opportunity to venture to a foreign land, I turned to ask my parents if I could go. To my surprise, they said yes. I began to daydream about this sojourn, wondering what I would pack, what I might see and how long I would be gone. Moments later my mother interrupted my fantasy by stating, 'You do know they're going to Brazil, Indiana, don't you?' Unsurprisingly, a trip to the county seat of Clay County, Indiana, which was less than forty miles from our house in West Central Indiana, did not appeal to my sense of adventure and, accordingly, I declined the opportunity. To this day, I'm not sure if I have been to the city of Brazil, although I'm fairly certain I've traveled through it. I certainly don't recall seeing scantily clad dancers sambaing in a carnival parade the last time I traveled on US-40.

In the years following that disappointment, I have sought out opportunities to travel whenever possible. However, I have come to learn that I am not – nor do I want to be – the typical tourist. I am not likely to sign up for a package tour. I do not care about seeing every cathedral in Europe nor do I plan to take in a major league game in every baseball stadium in the USA. On the contrary, I am far more likely to plan a trip to the upstate of South Carolina to attend Bubbafest (which I have done) or to Montana to attend the Testicle Festival (which I have not done – yet). To my great delight, I am married to a woman who shares my love of ironic tourism. Together, we have ridden wooden roller coasters at Holiday World in Santa Claus, Indiana; walked around old Soviet statues in Grūto Parkas, Lithuania; visited Bobby Sands's grave in Belfast, Northern Ireland; wandered the streets of Ljubljana, Slovenia, for part of a day after I had given a presentation at a conference in Klagenfurt, Austria; drunk a sauerkraut slushy at Pierogi Fest in Whiting, Indiana; won underwear at Gospel Fest in Chicago; and eaten garlic ice cream in Mérida, Venezuela. Nonetheless, in our travels we have never opted for the traditional tour of any place. I guess we are just not the type to follow a guide who holds up a flag while walking backwards and telling us what we should see.

The reasons for traveling are as varied as travelers themselves. While my wife and I have not read or even consulted Patricia Schultz's (2003) *1,000 Places to See before You Die: A Traveler's Life List*, we have always consulted the internet to help us plan our next adventure. Moreover, we have been able to 'virtually' travel to many more locales. I am positive that we are not alone in how we research places to visit, whether physically or virtually. And yet I am still surprised by the paucity of research that exists on official tourism websites.

Part of the motivation for examining official tourism websites comes from a desire to understand why cities, states, regions, nations, etc. choose certain images and language(s) to promote themselves. With the advent of the world wide web, we have become increasingly more informed about places to visit and things to do once we are there. Perhaps if the city of Brazil, Indiana, which now has an official website (http://www.brazil.in.gov/), had done a better job of promoting itself in the early 1970s, I would have wanted to go there.

Richard W. Hallett
Chicago, IL

Here I sit on the steps of the US Capital, warmed by the view before me of the Washington Monument, the left half of the Lincoln Memorial peeking around the Monument, and, over the tree tops, two domes and a sleek, flat upper section of another building. To my left, another dome, but this one, by contrast, striated as it crowns blocks of stone, bumpy in texture, earthen in tan. Green trees. Orange flowers. People – varying in their shapes and colors and purposes – just as these landmarks are of their tourist milieu. Languages – varied, as well, and in number I cannot keep up with. DC dawns on an August Monday and I wonder what discourses tie us all – tourist, pilgrim, native, worker – together. Are we all centered on the place and not just in it? And, if we are, what of the place do we think, do we speak, do we sign? And, at this particular time in my life, how and why did we all get here?

The answer to this question invokes not a mode of transportation, nor a wish come true, but, because I am engaged in this text, consideration of the means through which these individuals found their way to this portico, in this Mall, in this city. Did they read about DC before deciding to visit? After deciding to visit? Did they explore the Web? Were they influenced by words, pictures, layouts, content? Did they become, and further want to become, a part of the narratives these tourism sites tell? Ah, the researcher – never leaving the research behind. For all of us who come to these historic sites as tourists, the Web might play a role in how, why, where, when. The near universality of pre-trip inquiry and the increase of Web accessibility, make these questions worthy of pondering. The presence of this text in my life, makes these questions – and their answers – an essentiality.

I am here with my family on a tour of DC – a mix of vacation, college information sessions, and for one of us, government business. Mostly, though, it's vacation. We blend in as tourists and yet, what does that mean? We wear shorts; a couple of us carry and persistently use cameras; we have the ever-present water bottles slung from our necks. A backpack made heavy by lunches and snacks and even more drinks hangs from Daddy's shoulder. We are sight-seeing-ready with confirmed letters of congressionally booked tours. My family is on one of those tours now; I am not. Someone's got to hold all the stuff outside if the others are to pass security and go inside. I eagerly volunteer to be the holder. It's a mom thing and it's an author-trying-to-meet-deadline thing. I need time to think – and write. I sit on these steps of the Capitol Building with six water bottles, six lunches, and one backpack that thankfully also holds the brochure on which I sketch out this foreword among the descriptions and diagrams of the National Gallery of Art Sculpture Garden. Small margins in which to consider the irony of how my tourist gear has prevented me from being a tourist, but has offered me the time to reflect.

The people or tourists I watch, I assume carry out their roles without much active thought about how, what or why. But we, the analysts, bask in the chance to analyze. Excuse me a minute – one of those tourists has asked me to take a picture of her and her group as they stand on the steps with the mall of monuments and museums behind them. I must frame this picture correctly. It will tell a story perhaps for years to come. Given-New. Real-Ideal. Vectors. What will the choices I have made in setting up this photograph say about these five women and their tour of DC? Will it be something significant or not really anything greater than 'Here we are at the Mall'? But what does that say? And why do we collect and share these photographs? Certainly, they help us recall where we have been and perhaps how we felt. They promote us; they help us construct an identity – who we are, where we have been, what is there where we were, too. That's the very focus of this text – not the tourist, but the destination. And not the actual physical destination, but that place as framed, as positioned on the world wide web.

This virtual journey had led us as authors to many locales to which we have literally 'flown by the seat of our pants' as we investigate tourism websites. It has also led us to appreciate how linguistic and visual texts function both through anchorage and relay (Barthes, 1978) to construct for a locale and for a traveler an identity. In the context of social constructionism, we are who we are because of and through our interactions with others and, by extension, with the texts they create and come to be defined through. We have been constructed anew through our research; we trust that through our text you will be as well.

Judith Kaplan-Weinger
Chicago, IL

Chapter 1
Introduction

> clearly the language of tourism will increasingly become a language
> of cyberspace. (Dann, 1996: 161)

Discourse of Tourism

Not surprisingly, given the spread and rising influence of technology, we find ourselves, some 12 years after Dann's prediction, exploring this very medium – the language or discourse of tourism on the world wide web. Our initial foray into this area of inquiry began a few years back when Rick began researching a trip to his second 'home' to visit his 'host family', that is, the family with whom he had lived while he was an English-language teaching fellow in Lithuania in the mid-1990s. Unlike research in the 1990s, which would have been conducted primarily through traditional texts, e.g. printed travel guides and maps, Rick initiated this research by turning to the internet. He didn't have to go any further than the homepage of the official Lithuanian tourism site to find a 'rich point' (Agar, 1996), which has led us into the 'culture'/'grammar' of tourism websites. Here we are, a few years later, still immersed in the investigation of these sites, having traveled to numerous nations and cities, transported not through the planes, trains, buses, cars and legs that move the traditional tourist, but rather through the lexical and visual texts that populate websites and transport the (post-)modern traveler. As Dann explains,

> Via static and moving pictures, written texts and audio-visual offerings, the language of tourism attempts to persuade, lure, woo and seduce millions of human beings, and, in so doing, convert them from potential into actual clients. By addressing them in terms of their own culturally predicated needs and motivations, it hopes to push them out of the armchair and on to the plane – to turn them into tourists. Later, the language of tourism gently talks to them about the possible factors or attractions of competing destinations. Thus, since much of the rhetoric is both logically and temporally prior to any

travel or sightseeing, one can legitimately argue that tourism is grounded in discourse. (Dann, 1996: 2)

Why Websites?

Many contexts exist for examining the role of language and other semiotic modalities in the new capitalism (see Chouliaraki & Fairclough, 1999); these modalities are understood as mediators of social concerns and of social action in response to those concerns. One such context is tourism discourse – the content and modalities through which nations promote themselves or are promoted. As Gilbert (1999: 281) maintains, 'Conventional histories of tourism associate the development of the modern guidebook with the growth of mass tourism'. The role of these guidebooks should not be underestimated; for example, as Jack and Phipps (2005: 78) state, 'Travel guides are written and consumed with the intention of freeing the modern subject for travel. They have *emancipatory* potential and are framed as such' (emphasis added). Indeed, tourism researchers have often centered their research on the guidebooks; 'The guidebook is a crucial part of the touristic process, because it mediates the relationship between tourist and destination, as well as the relationship between host and guest' (Bhattacharya, 1997: 372). In the past, one might have said that journeys of thousands of miles do not begin with a single step. Today they begin with the guidebook; 'Reading travel guides is part of the process of preparation and anticipation. It enables the imagining of the destination. It is future-oriented travel in the present' (Jack & Phipps, 2005: 82). For Pritchard and Morgan (2005: 94), as well as many others, this 'future-oriented travel in the present' is not limited to guidebooks: 'Brochures, travel guides and *websites* available to tourists shape their expectations long before they arrive at their destination. Thus, the representations of local life presented in those texts become the codified and authorised versions of local culture and history' (emphasis added).

One manifestation of tourist discourse exists in travel guidebooks of the sort produced by Fodor's, Michelin and Lonely Planet, among a host of others. For some researchers, travel guidebooks show evidence of doctrinal 'truths'; e.g. Laderman (2002: 89) claims, 'Analyses in Western guidebooks reflect their construction by authors and editors who draw on original scholarship subscribing to disciplinary paradigms'. Additionally, as Baider *et al.* (2004: 27) note, 'The discourse of tourist guides, in its most general context, seemingly a site for the country to be visited to present itself, is in fact a place where the country of the author is also unfailingly inscribed in the glance which discursively *defines* this country' (original emphasis). This tourism discourse, according to Gilbert (1999: 282), 'has been seen as a key element in the development of the modern figure of the "tourist", following a prescribed route through a landscape of selected and ready-interpreted sites and monuments'.

The above claims can also be made in respect to a more recent addition to the body of tourism texts – world wide web sites produced by official government bodies to promote their respective nations and communities as appropriate locales for the tourist. As Rojek explains,

> With new communication technologies the individual is clearly an active participant in indexing and dragging. Personal computers with e-mail facilities enable the individual to combine elements from fictional and factual representational files. The practice might be described as *collage tourism*. That is, fragments of cultural information are assembled by the network user to construct a distinctive orientation to a foreign sight. (Rojek, 1997: 62, original emphasis)

In our post-Modern world '...the post-tourist finds it less and less necessary to leave home; technologies... allow people to "gaze" on tourist sites without leaving home' (Ritzer & Liska, 1997: 102).

Distinguishing two forms of traveling by readers, the ocular and the epistemic, Cronin (2000: 37) explains: 'Ocular travelling involves being transported to a place and being made to imagine that one is eye-witness at the countless scenes described by travel writers... Epistemic travelling can be expressed as the readers being persuaded to leave behind the safe berth of received opinion and to explore elements of their own or other cultures that they take for granted or of which they are ignorant'. For us, official tourism websites differ from travel writing in that, with their use of linguistic texts and visual texts, they allow for concurrent ocular and epistemic travel. Our analyses of these websites then, in recognition of the existing dearth of such research, are both timely and significant.

Why English?

While we hope the question of why we are exploring websites has been sufficiently addressed, we realize another question may exist – why English-language websites exclusively? Our answer is, initially, quite simple – we are native English speakers living in the USA, and while fully appreciating and thoroughly embracing the wealth of language varieties in which text exists on various tourism websites, we do not possess the necessary linguistic or communicative competence in these varieties to adequately explore the language used on these sites. Phipps (2007: 11) explains that the ties between language and tourism parallel those between language and all cultural domains – 'languages are seen as both fashioned and as being fashioned by tourist users and by those they encounter'. Therefore, this dynamic relationship both requires and deserves to be analyzed by those who can bring an emic approach to the undertaking. In sum, as Phipps (2007: 24) notes, 'no languages come with innocent histories but they are carriers of cultural legacies and tourists, as language carriers and language makers, are themselves embedded in an ongoing process of telling and writing of other cultures and other experiences, in and through languages'. We trust our analyses of English-language websites (some of which exist as one or two or more alternative language sites for a given locale) will inform the research of the language(s) of tourism. At the same time, we necessarily and enthusiastically encourage others to pursue analyses of these sites in order to add to the understanding of the role of language in the construction and promotion of identity, as well as in the growth of economic strength, collective pride and (inter)national awareness of a given nation or community. What may be 'lost in the translation' when attempting to analyze and understand a community's identity through an analysis of a language into which it has been translated, deserves to be noted. The ties between language and identity are as relevant in the investigation of websites as in any other pursuit in the context of a relativistic perspective. Concentration on English-language texts to the exclusion of others may, perhaps inadvertently, create a hegemonic structure whereby, as Cronin (2000: 86) explains, 'Not only do the guide books deliver the travellers to the same places the world over but the language of guide books creates a sensation of linguistic homogeneity'. Both comforting and troubling, such homogeneity may serve to unite yet simultaneously disregard linguistic and cultural diversity.

Outline of the Text

This book provides analyses of various tourism websites using the above theories. Drawing data from tourism websites for the countries of Latvia, Estonia, Lithuania and Myanmar (Burma); the state of Louisiana (USA); the cities of Santiago de Compostela (Spain), New Orleans (USA), Gary (USA); US Sports Halls of Fame; and the fictitious nations of Molvania, Phaic Tan and San Sombrero, this text variously examines the following:

(1) Official governmental tourism websites that promote independent identities for nations and often construct historical narratives for their nations.

(2) Communities that utilize their official tourism websites to serve as calls for action, such as by encouraging a pilgrimage to or participation in the rebirth of a particular place.
(3) Official tourism websites that strike a balance between promoting tourism while shielding potential travelers from danger.
(4) Official tourism websites that construct and promote identity through the use of metaphor, leading viewers to assign values associated with the metaphor to the locale itself.
(5) Parodic versions of tourism websites that capitalize on both the official tourism website genre and Western perceptions of the Other; though their content is fictitious, they (re)present the notion of Self and Other by reinforcing stereotypes of what it means to be hegemonic and central (as opposed to exotic and peripheral).

The discourse of tourism is a discourse of identity construction, promotion, recognition and acceptance. It is a discourse created through the creation and manipulation of linguistic and visual texts. Although these texts are specific to their locale and to those responsible for the respective websites on which they appear, they share common goals that become transparent through the work of discourse analysis. Those goals involve both producer and audience, both Self and Other, for no one is exempt from the affect of discourse. We are all impressionable; we are all malleable; we are all able, and most of us willing, to be touched by a text or an image. That a given text exists is evidence of both a given identity and a process of identity construction. That a range of like texts exist with the same goals in mind and the same outcomes as a result is no surprise, but rather is the observable evidence of the cultural norms for participation in and interpretation of interaction — norms dependent on cultural schema. van Leeuwen explains,

> Evidence of the existence of a given discourse comes from texts, from what has been said or written – and/or expressed by means of other semiotic modes. More specifically it comes from the similarity between things that are said and written in *different* texts about the *same* aspect of reality. It is on the basis of such similar statements, repeated or paraphrased in different texts and dispersed among these texts in different ways, that we can reconstruct the knowledge which they represent. (2005: 95, original emphasis)

Chapter 2
Identity and the World Wide Web: Methods of Analysis

The theoretical and methodological basis for this analysis is a mixture of theoretical perspectives, including social constructionism (Carbaugh, 1996), critical discourse analysis (CDA) (Wodak *et al.*, 1999), mediated discourse analysis (Scollon, 2001) and multimodal discourse analysis (Kress & van Leeuwen, 2001). These perspectives share a concern for studying language as social action and viewing social problems as 'inextricably linked to texts' (Schiffrin, 2004: 96). The world wide web, with its invitation to explore both within and outside the site through various links, encourages interaction between text and tourist. It serves, therefore, as a setting for the initiation and incitement of social action.

Johnstone (2002: 223) states, 'Discourse analysts have found the idea of performance useful in understanding how aspects of personal identity such as gender, ethnicity, and regional identification are connected to discourse'. Just as an individual performs a self, so can places. According to Wodak *et al.*, the practice of constructing national identity relies on a variety of methods for analyzing the 'narration of national culture' (Hall, 1996), including what they identify as strategies of using 'lexical units and syntactic devices which serve to construct unification, unity, sameness, difference, uniqueness, origin, continuity, gradual or abrupt change, autonomy, heteronomy and so on' (Wodak *et al.*, 1999: 35). Previously, we have shown how official governmental websites capitalize on this process of identity construction to promote their communities to potential tourists (Hallett & Kaplan-Weinger, 2004a, 2004b, 2006). In support, Jaworski and Thurlow (2004: 297) write, 'tourism can be viewed as an identity resource for members of post-industrial, late-modern societies'.

Identity construction most typically revolves around a nation or an individual characterizing a self by associating certain features with that self, and by disassociating that self from other features from which it wants to be viewed as distinct (cf. Mead, 1934; Morley & Robbins, 1995; Harré & van Langehove, 1999). Due to the role of language and, by extension, other semiotic modes in constructing and displaying a self, an analysis of national identity construction must incorporate a multimodal

6

analysis of the ways in which national identities are mediated (Scollon, 2001) through text – both linguistic and visual.

Because, as Scollon (2001: 11) explains, 'our social world is in fact a discursive social world', we can look at linguistic and visual texts as mediators in the process of 'solving the problem' of constructing a national identity. Specifically, for this text, we can look to tourism websites – their words **and** images – for how they mediate the social construction of independent communities. As a social action, the social construction of an independent identity is undertaken and, therefore, analyzed using a multimodal approach. As such, these websites make 'meaning in multiple articulations' (Kress & van Leeuwen, 1996: 4).

Critical Discourse Analysis

The field originating in linguistics that considers language as a social phenomenon and thus analyses texts and places these texts in their context in order to determine the function of the discourse they represent in society is called Critical Discourse Analysis (CDA). More than just linguistics, CDA is an interdisciplinary approach with a linguistic basis. Indeed, CDA aims to investigate social inequalities as they are constituted, expressed and transmitted by language; and the three most important concepts in CDA are power, history and ideology. (Le, 2006: 13)

In the context of CDA, the functions of tourism are social actions, i.e. attempts to (1) socially construct and promote communities as significant to the individual's, the city's and the world's well-being; and (2) (re)construct nations and other communities by variably fostering re-imagining, rebirth, renaissance, promotion and caution, and patriotism (Wodak *et al.*, 1999). According to Locke (2004: 2), CDA 'views reality as textually and intertextually mediated via verbal and non-verbal language systems, and texts as sites for both the inculcation and contestation of discourses'. Such systems, especially as they compose world wide web sites, are one set of channels through which the identity work of tourism texts is accomplished. Social actions are manifested and mediated (Scollon, 2001) in tourism through official world wide web sites created by governmental bodies to promote tourism. As these sites encourage tourism, through multimodal texts (Kress & van Leeuwen, 2001), they also construct and promote for their communities an identity as a welcoming, soothing, (divinely) poignant setting for spiritual, intellectual and cultural fulfillment. Echoed by Robinson and Smith,

Each nation, no matter what their [sic] position in any notional global political league table, promotes tourism as an actual and potential source of external revenue, a marker of political status that draws upon cultural capital, and as a means to legitimise itself as a territorial entity. Thus, national governments have offices for tourism that quite willingly promote the idea of a national "brand". (Robinson & Smith, 2006: 2)

Mediated Discourse Analysis

In recent years, advances in technology have made it possible to discover and explore a locality before one physically travels to it. In particular, the world wide web, in allowing interaction between tourist and locality, has come to play a mediational role not only in the tourist experience, but also in the co-construction of tourist identities. This text examines this role by applying linguistic and visual design theory to the analysis of travel websites – the content and structure of which reveal much about the activity/place/identity dialectic of these sites and the social construction of the tourists' (and, as we will discuss later, pilgrims') identities. At the same time, this text focuses on/recognizes the nascent position of the world wide web as an ideological mediator of tourism. Linguistic and visual texts present meaning on both denotative and connotative levels. These texts do not just communicate; they represent and mediate. They are negotiative and dialogic. As Web users move through hypertext, they participate in the co-constructional process of identity formation. Therefore, as Hannam and Knox (2005: 23) assert, 'Discourse analysis should thus treat any textual or visual data as mediated cultural products which are part of wider systems of knowledge. Utilizing discourse analysis should mean the development of a more nuanced reading of textual data and thus add a more critical edge to much tourism research'.

In this era of globalization, in which national identities are increasingly constructed through promotion reflecting growth and change as much as tradition and convention, texts – both linguistic and visual – occupy a seminal role. Analyses of these texts have variably illustrated that tourism, to quote Dann (1996: 2), 'in the act of promotion, as well as in the accounts of its practitioners and clients, has a discourse of its own'. For some researchers, e.g. MacCannell and Urry, this discourse is tantamount to 'dystopian tales of the subject under Modernity' (Jack & Phipps, 2005: 16). Nonetheless, there still exists a paucity of research on this discourse (cf. Jaworski & Pritchard, 2005; Phipps, 2007; *inter alia*).

As promotion of nationalism has increased, so has the recognition that tourism can be a decisive force in nation building and the identity construction of these nations. Numerous analyses have recently centered on this function of tourism, pointing out that tourism promotes 'international familiarisation/normalisation' as well as 'cosmopolitanism' (Urry, 1995: 166). In fact, tourism and nationalism often go hand in hand: 'The recent period has seen a global public stage emerging upon which almost all nations have to appear, to compete, to mobilise themselves as spectacle and to attract large numbers of visitors' (Urry, 2002: 158; see also Roche, 2000). To promote tourism is not only to engage in the new capitalism (Fairclough, 1992), but also to engage in identity construction (see Robinson & Smith, 2006).

Destinations for tourists are simultaneously homes for their inhabitants. Sometimes, these residents make their living through their service to these tourists. Tourism, along with offering educational and recreational benefits, has its economic rewards in the short and long term. Tourists leave with artifacts and memories that compose stories. Stories breed more tourists who bring in more money. This cycle is vital to the internal growth, external recognition and identity construction of the host community, as well as to the sustenance and pride of its inhabitants. From tourism, communities reap the positive political benefits of an increased world presence. Yet, this world hosts a wide variety of communities that make their ways through life distinctly. While tourism offers opportunities for construction and promotion, thereby buttressing the campaign of any nation to gain equal status as a political entity and a tourist destination, not all communities are the same; therefore, not all communities are similarly affected by outsiders and their contributions – economic, cultural and the like. Additionally, not all communities welcome the benefits when weighed against the detriments of a tourism industry. In this era of increased opportunities to tour and increased numbers of communities to tour, it is quite relevant to examine increased means for spreading and retrieving information about these opportunities. In this text, those means are official (i.e. government-sponsored) tourism internet websites, texts in which, according to Castells (2000) in his analysis of the relationship between technology and economic growth, the communication of an experience itself becomes an experience. Castells (2000:4) explains the importance of understanding that this real virtuality works in a 'binary mode' such that the messages presented can be 'changed, transformed, or even subverted' by those with whom they interact. Similarly, as Cronin explains,

When we talk about global flows, we mean, of course, not only the physical displacement of human beings and physical objects but also the transfer of information in the virtual world of cyberspace. The migration of information to other sites, where languages other than the language in which the material originated are used, brings with it the necessity for and the challenge of localization. Localization indeed is frequently hailed as a means of protecting linguistic specificity and cultural difference. (Cronin, 2006: 28)

The role of technology as a mediator in the creation of communities of practice, such as sacred 'pilgrims' and secular tourists who interact with the real virtuality of a website, is supported by Barthes' (1978) concept of a 'writerly text' in which a reader/viewer is able to choose his/her relation to a text by using different links and networks of information to negotiate a path through the text. Liestøl (1994: 87) echoes this idea as he explains how hypertext reconfigures our conception of texts: 'The facilities of manipulation, individual navigation, and freedom from given, authoritative structures provide us with new practices of writing and reading'. In hypertext, the networks are many and interact, and through their interactional structure and through a reader's interpretation of this structure, provide an opportunity for the reader/user to socially construct a self as a knowledgeable and experienced traveler before setting a physical foot in the locale. Hypertext, then, is a vital contribution to the function of websites as constructors of identity through the promotion of social action. Therefore, as Bhattacharya (1997: 381) explains, 'While a guidebook shapes the images of the destination through both selection of sights and providing information about them, it is the process of interpretation that is perhaps most crucial in this regard. Interpretation is a combination of contextualization and evaluation'. Interpretation is a process of interaction.

Multimodal Discourse Analysis: Linguistic and Visual Texts

In previous research on the role of the world wide web in constructing the national, independent identity of Lithuania, we have argued that an analysis of the construction of identity/identities must focus multimodally on how identity is mediated and negotiated through websites (Hallett & Kaplan-Weinger, 2004a). Multimodal discourse analysis, incorporating both visual semiotic analysis and CDA, offers researchers a range of texts on which to conduct the study of identity construction.

Through analysis that focuses on visual semiotics and visual design as well as linguistics, we find that a multimodal approach allows a fuller exploration of the discursive formation and promotion of identity. Traditional semiotic analysis, with its focus on the sign – its signifier and its signified – provides a starting point for the multimodal analysis of tourism websites. According to Barthes (1978: 14), any sign must be seen to have both a denotative and a connotative signified. In a denotative interpretation, the mode 'transmit[s]... the scene itself, the literal reality'. In a connotative interpretation, the modes instead transmit 'the manner in which the society to a certain extent communicates what it thinks' (Barthes, 1978: 17). More recently, theories of social semiotics, visual semiotics, visual design, multimodal discourse analysis and mediated discourse analysis have taken on the analysis of text and image. Explained by van Leeuwen and Jewitt (2001: 3), the mutual goal of such research (though approached in varying ways) is to provide a 'detailed and explicit method for analysing the meanings established by the syntagmatic relations between the people, places, and things depicted in images. These meanings are described as not only representational, but also interactional (images do things to or for the viewer)'. Necessary to acknowledge, in conducting such analysis, is that, as elucidated by Pritchard and Morgan (2005: 57), '...understanding and interpreting any visual image is highly complex and the issues of "representation", "trustworthiness", "interpretation", "reflexivity" and "sampling" are all highly contested in visual research'.

The post-modernist view of social constructionism positions the viewer to look at and interpret an image in a variety of ways – various signifieds are promoted through interpretations of various signifiers. Interestingly, in their respective analyses of tourists and tourism, both Rojek and Urry (1997) and Jack and Phipps (2005) characterize tourists as 'semioticians'; the latter expanding on that positioning by describing tourists as 'ordering and producing and affecting their experiences in historical, economic, social, cultural and visual ways' (Jack & Phipps, 2005: 67). Visual and linguistic texts have meaning potential – particular meanings are interpreted through the interaction of texts, their creators, their settings and their interpreters. Application of visual semiotic analysis to tourism websites identifies further efforts by websites at social construction of identity through selection and inclusion of particular photographs. In fact, as Hannam and Knox stress,

The value of semiotic analysis is in the fact that it recognizes that there are usually several layers of meaning within any textual or visual analysis and that these are usually arbitrary but bound by particular cultural contexts. Thus, a semiotic approach encourages greater depth of analysis beyond the obvious or the literal to reveal the indirect and often unintentional levels of meaning in any text. (2005: 25)

(For more on semiotics, see van Leeuwen, 2005.) Furthermore, as Royce (2007: 67) explains, 'Visuals, *inter alia*, are representations of reality, or representations of experience and information, and in that sense they realize the ideational metafunction, where patterns are represented'.

Travel as Metaphor: Websites as Narratives

Interpretation of meaning depends on one's conceptual system. As such, analytic attention needs to be paid to the use of linguistic and visual texts not only to socially construct identity and inspire one to social action, but also to activate schema. One salient discourse strategy made use of in many travel websites is metaphor. In the context of travel websites, metaphor is a narrative device. As we become more accustomed to the metaphor of life as story, we come to view our lives as perpetually-constructed narratives. As Aristotle noted in his *Poetics* (XXII), 'The greatest thing in style is to have command of metaphor'. However, metaphor is more than just a stylistic issue; we come to understand that our life stories are not composed by us alone, but are the product of dynamic, life-long interaction with others. Among the contributors to our life stories are our actions and interactions during travel events. Travel exists ideologically in the USA (and presumably in other places as well) as a belief in the value of 'getting away from it all', of 'experiencing other worlds', of 'broadening our horizons'. These values are themselves prompted by the search for leisure, relaxation, fun and/or education – each an accepted reason for and outcome of travel. Operating as a grand narrative, the ideology of travel and tourism guides the selection of places to go, things to see and do, and even of memories to make and later to recall. Along with one's desire to be a part of and conform to this narrative is one's always constant shaping and reshaping of his or her identity. In the post-modern view of identity as a social construct, travel and tourism can be seen as one way to participate in a 'social relationship' (MacCannell, 1999) and to fulfill the desire 'to share an intimate connection between one stranger and another, or one generation to another, through the local object [and to establish] a certain kind of human solidarity' (MacCannell, 1999: 203).

Traditionally defined, metaphor is based on a resemblance between the two identities that are compared and identified. Lakoff and Johnson (1980), however, say that there need not be similarities between the entities. They hold that metaphor helps us understand the world, conceptualize the world, make sense of reality. The interpretation of meaning, then, depends on one's conceptual system. Therefore, with metaphor incorporated into Web texts, there exists the opportunity to analyze these texts as illustrative of linguistic relativism.

Conclusion

As government agencies employ websites to promote tourism to their nations and cities, they serve as mediators of a multimodal array of systems structured with content intended to attract both the interest of and economic input from tourists. In their attempts at self-promotion, such agencies engage in what may be understood as a form of 'autoethnography' – defined by Buzard (2001: 300, adapted from Pratt, 1992), as 'the authoritative representation of "ourselves," or "our" landscape, traditions, and way of life'. Our 'tours' through these sites provide the tourist with the chance not only to be somewhere other than where we are, but to be someone other than who we are. Our identity is in flux as our travels – virtual or actual – remove us from one location and place us in another. And with this, we are quite comfortable; the very 'language' of the web is the language of the tourist. Our tourist identity is constructed as we use the internet, not only through the sites we visit, but also the actions in which we engage. As Franklin explains,

> we surf like tourists and the web is set up in a tourist way. Take the language of the web for a start. We "visit" web "sites". We wander around the sites as the mood takes us, leisurely or erratically; sites provide us with "maps" and when we arrive anywhere we are given "itineraries", "menus", "gateways", "access". It is a language of movement, "back", "forward", "go", "stop", and so on. There is also something touristic about the way sites are constructed; they aim to attract us, make us linger, entertain us and of course sell us something. The web is our virtual world and it is just as we like it: constantly changing. We are now like tourists all the time; we are restless, addicted to motion, itching to set off. We seem to inhabit many places simultaneously. (2003: 8)

Our particular journey, in this text, will focus on the words and pictures of tourism – the discourses created by and for a nation, its habitants and its visitors. Hummon (1988: 181) asserts that, 'As a ritual text, tourist advertising is involved in a symbolic transformation of reality, remaking ordinary places – from New York to Iowa – into extraordinary tourist worlds.' Through the discourses of tourism, all creators and all that is created find their identities transformed, constructed anew through the creation and promotion of their locale and, ultimately as well, through interaction with those who visit, either virtually or concretely. The discourse of tourism makes an especially valid source for the analysis of identity construction of both destinations and those whom they attempt to attract. Edensor (2002: 84–85) explains that 'As tourism becomes the world's largest industry, national tourism strategies increasingly seek to compete in this global market by advertising their distinct charms; trying to carve out a unique niche that might attract the "golden hordes"'. It is these strategies we now move to explore.

Chapter 3

Narrative of the Nation: Baltic Tourism Websites in the Post-Soviet Context

Introduction

In the context of what Fairclough (1992) identifies as 'language in the new capitalism', a concern of discourse analysts is how lexical and visual texts construct and confirm the 'new order'. Fairclough's claim that 'the project of the new order is partly a language project', fits quite well within the theoretical and analytical framework of critical discourse analysis, which views language as a call to social action. As independent nations, Lithuania, Latvia and Estonia, following the dismantling of the Soviet Union, must construct their identities anew. One way they have each chosen to do so is through the promotion of themselves as tourist destinations through the world wide web. As noted earlier, identity construction most typically revolves around a nation or other locale characterizing a self through both association and disassociation. This characterization is produced in part through both multimodal and mediational means.

History

Lithuanian, Latvian, and Estonian have continued to exist as the primary languages of their respective nations despite foreign occupation and campaigns to promote other national languages. For example, the Russian tsarist government, which controlled all three Baltic states until 1918, instituted a policy of russification and banned the Latin script. Nevertheless, all three titular languages were maintained, often covertly, primarily because of the connection between language loyalty and national identity. During the Second World War, these states were occupied first by the Soviet Union, then by the Third Reich, and then, again, following the Second World War, by the Soviet Union. All three nations gained their independence from the Soviet Union in 1990.

Linguistic and Visual Texts in the Social Construction of National Identity

The efforts of the Baltic nations in their state of post-Soviet independence provide an introduction to the role of hypertext in the social construction of national identity. Their respective official tourism websites serve as mediators of this social action, with their respective linguistic and visual texts serving dialectically to aid in these nations' (re)definition of themselves for both their citizens and the world beyond their borders. The Baltic tourism websites that are analyzed in this chapter serve to illustrate how multimodal texts function as mediators in the social construction of national independence.

To adapt a multimodal discourse analysis perspective to this analysis of identity construction, we must understand that 'Discourses are socially constructed knowledge of (some aspect of) reality... [T]hey have been developed in specific social contexts, and in ways which are appropriate to the interest of social actors in these contexts' (Kress & van Leeuwen, 1996: 4). Who are the social actors who interact with these websites and together with their creators construct an independent identity for the nation they promote? Three of the actors are the creators of the sites – the Lithuanian Tourist Board, a government institution that 'formulates and implements the policy of the government in the area of tourism' (www.randburg.com/li/lithtourist.html); the Latvian Tourism Development Agency, which 'implements state policy in the field of tourism and promotes tourism development in Latvia' (www.varam. gov.lv/varam/P_inst/Eltaa.htm); and the Estonian Tourist Board, which, among its goals, are 'Marketing Estonia as a tourism destination; [c]oordination of tourism development programmes; [and c]oordination of tourism research and analysis' (www.visitestonia.com/index.php? page = 42, accessed 21/11/09).

Another set of actors is tourists – perhaps Baltic natives, perhaps individuals having ancestral ties to these places, perhaps those who want to make the Baltic states a locale for the enjoyment and study of nature and history. We cannot speak to the intentions of those who created the sites and their motives in choosing which language or languages, which texts or which visual images to incorporate. We can, however, within theories of mediated and multimodal discourse analysis, speak to the effects these sites and their linguistic and visual modes and content may have on at least some of their users.

The websites for the Lithuanian State Department of Tourism[1] (LSDT), the Latvian Tourism Development Agency (LTDA) and the Estonian

Tourist Board serve as the main sources of information on Lithuanian, Latvian and Estonian tourism websites. All examples given in this chapter exist or existed originally on these sites or on sites linked to these sites. In some cases, the original linguistic and visual text no longer appear on these websites, but are still found on other internet sites. Under the auspices of the Ministry of the Economy of the Republic of Lithuania, the LSDT is responsible for drafting governmental proposals on tourism policy and marketing Lithuanian tourism (LSDT website, par. 1; Randburg website, par. 7). The LSDT website provides information on various Lithuanian facts and services and has links to nineteen different tourism information centers' websites, sixteen links to Lithuanian tour operators' websites and three links to tourism organizations' websites, among others. Under the Ministry of Environment of the Republic of Latvia, the LTDA not only maintains an information database on Latvian tourism, but also disseminates domestic and international tourism information and conducts market research (LTDA website, par. 1). This website has thirty links to various pages containing information about Latvia, from communications to folklore, and has specific information about six regions of Latvia. The Estonian tourism website similarly links to an array of sites with information related to places and activities and offers an online version of its 24-page, glossy, full-colored travel guide. The analysis of these respective websites reveals that Lithuanian, Latvian and Estonian national identities are both generated by and promoted through linguistic and visual content.

The Social Construction of Independent Identity: Language Choice

The fact that the official websites of the Baltic nations primarily use English to promote tourism is not surprising given the status of English as a language of widespread communication. Additionally, the presence of English connotes the interest these nations have in attracting English speakers, including Lithuanian-, Latvian- and Estonian-Americans, to their respective homelands. When we first began our research of the official Baltic tourism websites, back in 2002, the English language was predominant on these sites. For example, the LSDT offered only two languages – English and Lithuanian. At that time, all the websites linked to the main LSDT website offered English and all but two came up first in English. Today, one of the links to the LSDT website, www.travel.lt, offers six language choices on its homepage: in order, Lithuanian, English, Russian, German, Polish and Italian. Similarly, in 2003, the homepage offered Latvia, English and Russian, but at that time the Russian link was not accessible. No other languages were offered at that time on the Latvian tourism websites. Today, however, the LTDA homepage offers access to Latvian, English, Russian, German, Lithuanian, Estonian, French, Polish, Italian, Finnish, Swedish and Spanish. Likewise, the official tourism website for Estonia, www.visitestonia.com, offers, in order, English, Finnish, Russian, German, Estonian and Japanese.

Even though each of these nations is fiercely proud of its national language, all three appeal to English as a means of communication most likely because of its status as an international language. However, they don't position other languages of wider communication as they do English. Speakers of any of the Baltic languages could use their European neighbors' languages, but they choose not to. This is most likely because English doesn't carry the negative baggage that some other languages do, e.g. German and Russian. In the Baltics, English is not considered to be an imperialist language because no English-speaking nation or government has ever controlled them. Their inclusion of English on their respective websites indicates a desire to identify with the English-speaking world. As Wright (2000: 56) explains, 'In the Baltic States the tension between the Balts and the Russians is not caused by linguistic difference; it is, of course, the result of power relationships between the conquerors and the conquered. Nevertheless, language is important because it is the salient marker that defines the groups'.

The Social Construction of Independent Identity: Linguistic Texts

As we demonstrated in Hallett and Kaplan-Weinger (2004a), national identity construction can be a product of the 'narration of national culture' (Hall, 1996) and strategies in the use of 'lexical units and syntactic devices which serve to construct unification, unity, sameness, difference, unique-ness, origin, continuity, gradual or abrupt change, autonomy, heteronomy and so on' (Wodak *et al.*, 1999). To this end, we first apply Hall's (1996) model to the Baltic nation websites to illustrate how they have employed linguistic texts to construct their nascent independent identities. Evidence of the use or the narration of national culture is found on each of the official Baltic websites and their respective links. The examples that follow are illustrative not only of Hall's (1996) claims, but also of Wodak *et al.*'s (1999) extended model that accounts for linguistic structures functioning to construct autonomous national identities.

Hall's (1996) model states that the construction of national identity can be the result of (a) a narrative of the nation; (b) an emphasis on origins, continuity, traditions and timelessness; (c) an invention of tradition; (d) a foundation of myth of origin; and (e) a pure, original people or 'folk'. Example (3.1), from the official Estonian tourism website, illustrates how narrative serves to assign historicity and, therefore, legitimacy, to a nation and to its complementary claim to an autonomous existence.

> (3.1) Estonians have been living in this tiny portion of the Baltic lands since approximately 2,500 B.C., making them the longest settled of the European peoples. Due to Estonia's strategic location as a link between East and West, it has been highly coveted through the ages by rapacious kings and conquerors. (www.visitestonia.com/index. php?page = 61, accessed 9/1/08)

Examples such as (3.1), which again occur on all the Baltic tourism websites, capitalize on the strength of the given regions to withstand the military interests of invading nations – to fend off outsiders and maintain both their sense and presentation of an independent self. Building on Hall's and Wodak *et al.*'s claims, we argue that the presentation of the narration of a nation is salient on these official websites as it establishes a legitimate extended history for the people who have remained and retain ties to this region, irrespective of governments ruling through occupation.

Example (3.2) highlights the use of images of stability and permanence in structuring a narrative of a nation. The tourism websites make use of these kinds of examples to emphasize – in Hall's terminology – origins, continuity, traditions, and timelessness.

> (3.2) First settlements of Latvian ancestors along the Baltic coast are dated from 2500 BC. Seriously about settlement in territory of today's Riga we can talk only by the time when this area was important ancient pitch of amber export [sic]. Then this place was important as a strategically convenient location in the estuary of the Daugava big waterway, amidst the ancient root "from Vikings to Greeks" (also called the Amber Way). (www.latviatourism.lv/defmenu/ievads.php? raj_id = 51, accessed 18/3/03) and (www.latvianembassy.org.cn/en/ culture/.htm, accessed 9/1/08)

This example, from the Latvian tourism site, highlights the long history of Riga as a commercial port. Its use of 'ancestors' and 'ancient' (twice), reinforces the continuity of the city and, therefore, of the Latvian nation.

Example (3.3), which we have discussed in Hallett and Kaplan-Weinger (2004a: 222), can be found at the Biržai link on the Lithuanian website. It illustrates the third aspect of Hall's model – invention of tradition.

(3.3) Near the village of Kirkiali, a gypsy drowned with his horse and wagon in a sudden sinkhole. In another famous case, a farmer awoke to find his cow missing. The cow was swallowed up by the now famous "Hole of the Cow." At the bottom of the hole is a small, dark passage leading to an underground cavern, which is about 46 meters long, and a small, underground lake that's a meter and a half deep. To get to the cow hole, driving from Pabirže to Biržai, turn left at the sign "Karves Ola"—cow hole—and watch for more signs. (www.birzai.lt/index.php?id = 43&pg = .000001082.000003559&kid = 1&tev = 3559, accessed 9/1/08)

The tradition invented here accounts for the name of what has become a prominent tourist attraction. This example is particularly notable for its dependence on a folktale to suggest that one of Lithuania's strengths lies in its heritage.

Example (3.4), which we have also discussed previously (Hallett & Kaplan-Weinger, 2004a: 222) addresses the fourth component of Hall's model – foundation of myth of origin.

(3.4) The present city name is traced to the word "šaulys" (the shot). People say that in the old days, the surrounding woods were abundant with wild beasts and birds, therefore, the hunters and the shots settlement [sic] on the bank of the lake was called Šiauliai. (www.siauilai.lt/tourism, accessed 15/2/02)

Here, the explanation for a Lithuanian city's origin is given. This example is significant not only for providing the etymology of the place name Šiauliai, but also for again establishing that people have lived and hunted there for centuries – even well before the founding of the city.

The last of Hall's components – pure, original people/'folk' – is also found on the official tourism websites. Example (3.5), which comes from the Lithuanian site, specifically states that Lithuania is the 'most indigenous' of the three Baltic countries based on its ethnic composition.

(3.5) **Ethnic Composition:** Lithuanians – 83.5%, Polish – 6.7%, Russians – 6.3%, Belarusians – 1.2%, others – 2.3%. Lithuania is home to as many as 115 ethnic groups. Based on ethnic composition, Lithuania is the most indigenous of all the Baltic countries.

(www.travel.lt/turizmas/selectPage.do?docLocator = 5747AOCF3E
DC11DA8A2B74616467373&inlanguage = en, accessed 9/1/08)

What makes Lithuania unique among the Baltic nations is its
overwhelmingly native population. In a similar vein, the Latvian website
also focuses on a segment of its population to establish a unique identity
for Latvia.

(3.6) The Kurzeme coastline is home for the ancient Livs. Their fight for
survival today is the subject of international scientific study. Of the 182
registered Livs, only about 10 still speak the Livi language—the least
number of people to speak a unique language in Europe. (www.latvia
tourism.lv/defmeny/kurzeme_en.php, accessed 19/3/03) and (www.
travellatvia.lv/8/19/1444/en/?country = , accessed 9/1/08)

Highlighting knowledge shared by a minimal number of Latvians, the
site further distinguishes the nation from all others.

Focusing on the written texts of these websites, we can also use Wodak
et al.'s (1999) model for examples of the discursive construction of national
identity on the Lithuanian, Latvian and Estonian tourism websites. The
websites provide examples of singularization (3.7, 3.8, 3.9, 3.10); demontage, dismantling and discrediting pillars of identity/opponents (3.11,
3.12); and perpetuation and positive self-presentation (3.13, 3.14):

Singularization:
(3.7) Lithuania is the only Baltic country with nearly eight hundred
years of statehood tradition, while its name was first mentioned
almost one thousand years ago, in 1009. Wedged at the dividing line of
Western and Eastern civilizations, Lithuania battled dramatically for
its independence and survival. Once in the Middle Ages, Lithuania
was the largest state in the entire Eastern Europe, where crafts and
overseas trade prospered. (www.travel.lt/turizmas/selectPage.do?doc
Locator = 78FOAAA93EE211DA8A2B746164617373&inlanguage = en,
accessed 9/1/08)
(3.8) Lithuania is the geographical centre of Europe. In 1989, scientists
of National Geographic Institute of France gave the description of the
European geographic centre and, applying the scientific method of
gravitation centres, appointed that this centre is located in the North
from Vilnius (26 km), near Purnuskes village. (www.travel.lt/turiz
mas/selectPage.do?docLocator = 4BED58D2AA7D11D9838E7461646
17373&inlanguage = en&pathId = 296, accessed 9/1/08)
(3.9) Historic Centre of Riga, while retaining its medieval and later
urban fabric relatively intact, is of outstanding universal value by

virtue of the quality and quantity of its Art Noveau/Jugenstill architecture, which is unparalleled anywhere in the world. (www.lat viatourism.lv/defmenu/ievads.php?raj_id = 51, accessed 19/3/08) and (www.latvianembassy.org.cn/en/culture.htm, accessed 9/1/08) (3.10) The islands off the coast are virtual dreamlands, unlike anything in Europe. The two largest islands are Saaremaa and Hiiumaa, which are both retreats from faced-paced city life. The islands, which also include the smaller Muhu, Kihnu and Ruhnu, have a laid-back, friendly air about them. And the landscape is considered quintessentially Estonian, with many windmills, thatched cottages and sleepy fishing villages (www.visitestonia.com/index. php?page = 57, accessed 19/3/03) and (www.est-tours.co.uk/Stag_ Estonia_Tallinn_GroupHuntingandPrecision Shooting.aspx, accessed 9/1/08)

Demontage, Dismantling and Discrediting:
(3.11) After Soviet occupation caused by immigration of Russian-speaking persons the Latvian language was purposefully eradicated from official and social spheres. Russian language badly influenced Latvian language especially its mutual culture that was swamped by barbarisms and direct translations, phonetics and syntax were also affected. Meanwhile important foreign working and literature were adapted and translated, the Language and Literature Institute (present Latvian Language Institute of Latvian University) was established. Since 1988 Latvian Language re-established its main positions and is the official language of Latvia Republic. (www.latviatourism.lv/latvija/ valoda_en.php, accessed 19/3/03)
(3.12) The Republic of Estonia was declared on 24 February, 1918, and for a couple of decades the people felt pride in their home country, work, children and achievements. The vile and destructive occupation by the Soviet Union which lasted half a century interrupted the natural development of many spheres of life in Estonia, which until then had been keeping up well with its northern neighbour Finland. (www. visitestonia.com/index.php?page = 8, accessed 9/1/08)

Perpetuation and Positive Self-presentation:
(3.13) There are no words expressive enough to convey an authentic view of Latvia. That is why you should come here – you should see, hear, taste, and feel it all yourself. (www.latviatourism.lv/info. php?id = 48, accessed 9/1/08)
(3.14) This is not only a nation with a touching, visible past; it's a nation that is as progressive and hip as it is history-filled and quaint. Its

spectacular progress since restoring its independence in 1991 is epitomized by its impressive internet infrastructure, considered one of the most advanced anywhere in the world. Even in the depths of the countryside, you're almost as likely to see a villager surfing the internet as milking a cow. (www.visitestonia.com/index.php?page = 8, accessed 19/3/03) and (www.viabalticanordica.com/tourism/practicalinfo.html, accessed 9/1/08)

An analysis of linguistic texts focused on the ways in which they serve to construct identity is particularly significant in the case of communities attempting to regain an earlier-held independent identity. For Lithuania, Latvia and Estonia, countries whose political and social systems were challenged by their occupation by the Soviet Union, tourism affords opportunities for world recognition, economic advancement and national pride. This analysis continues below, though with a focus on visual texts, for how they, too, function to construct and promote independent national identity.

The Social Construction of Independent Identity: Visual Texts

Words, their denotative extension and connotative intension, convey meaning at multiple levels. Because, in a social constructionist framework, meaning is negotiated between speaker–listener, writer–reader and artist–viewer, the significance to any one person of any one sign is dependent on the interpretation made within the context in which the sign is produced. Among these contextual factors are the purported and implied goals of the speaker/writer/artist, the listener's/reader's/viewer's schema and the textual and social contexts in which the sign is presented. We have seen that in order to decode the meaning performed on these and other sites, it is necessary to go beyond the linguistic texts to include the visual texts. Therefore, our exploration of the Lithuanian and Estonian tourism websites turns now to the application of visual semiotic and visual design theory to complete a multimodal approach to the analysis of the discursive formation and promotion of national identity.[2]

People

In an earlier analysis, we argued that the relative absence of the people of Lithuania in the majority of visual texts on the Lithuanian tourism websites was reflective of how, during the pre-independent era, Lithuanians were hesitant to have photographs of themselves taken, less they be shown to be in locations or with people judged to be unfavorable by the ruling government. This pattern no longer exists on the Lithuanian tourism website. Perhaps in the intervening years, Lithuanians have become less hesitant; perhaps, more simply, more photographs are being taken and the proportion of people- to place-pictures has increased. Perhaps there is a political and/or social explanation; perhaps there is not. What there is now before us, with the increase in numbers of photographs on the travel.lt site as well as the photographs on the latviatourism.lv and visitestonia.com sites, is the opportunity to explore the visual semiotic of these Baltic sites in terms of both their people and places.

The following set of photographs, from the 'Historical and Architectural Heritage' link on the travel.lt site introduces the viewer to individuals and groups engaged in social and cultural interactions. The photographs of the procession at the Gates of Dawn (Photo 3.1) and the city festival (Photo 3.2) juxtapose traditional and contemporary Lithuania. The Gates of Dawn are the remains of a 17th-century shrine to the Virgin Mary; the city festival includes a parade participated in by a contemporary marching band and accompanying cheerleaders. What the photographs share is motion – the

Photo 3.1 The Gates of Dawn, Vilnius (www.travel.lt, accessed 11/3/09)

Photo 3.2 City festival, Lithuania (www.travel.lt, accessed 11/3/09)

central participants make their way along the most salient path – the middle of the road that leads out of the background and into the foreground. The viewer is positioned as receiver of the procession; in semiotic terms, as the distance between the members of the procession and the viewer decreases, the viewer's point of view changes as she/he becomes more engaged in the event. The images are still; no movement actually occurs. However, as onlooker, the viewer becomes a participant as the processions pass by. The viewer's involvement increases; the events become personalized. The viewer becomes a celebrant of the traditions and, therefore, part of the larger community of those who help maintain Lithuania's identity as an independent nation.

Children are salient in a number of photographs on these websites. In our earlier analysis (Hallett & Kaplan-Weinger, 2004a), Lithuanian children were pictured in a set of photographs at an orphanage (see, e.g. Photo 3.3). Gathered with one another or with their teachers, these children were positioned as a community; their proximity to one another in the context of their being orphans connoted their mutual need for one another and for their nation's support. An appeal to the potential tourist was also noticeable in their alignment through a horizontal vector directed from the children to the viewer as they pose for the photographer.

Other photographs on the current Lithuanian tourism site as well as the Latvian and Estonian sites also focus on children. In contrast to the

Photo 3.3 Trakai children's house, Trakai, Lithuania (www.travel.lt, accessed 15/2/02)

dominance of group photographs on the Lithuanian site previously analyzed, the sites accessed in 2009 also showcase a number of children alone or in much smaller groups. For example, found on a link called 'Latvia in Pictures/Children', a photograph places a young girl in salient position. Her gaze is directed up and to her left to given and ideal quadrants, suggesting her interaction with someone who is taller and older and to whom she 'can look up to' literally and figuratively. In her hand, the girl holds a cookie decorated as a horse. Her attire and hair are formalized. With the upward gaze, the girl presents a pleading self – one who perhaps wants to have the cookie and is waiting for the permission of the elder. Her mouth is closed, suggesting her silence and patience as she awaits the feedback she seeks. The viewer's eyes are drawn to hers – the blueness of her eyes stand out in contrast against the pink hue of her face and white wisps of hair on her face. The viewer is invited into such pictures and made a voyeur because, as Matthiessan (2007: 20) explains, 'Perspective and gaze work interpersonally in pictorial systems because they imply a location of the viewer in an extension of what is represented'.

Estonia, too, promotes itself as a place for children as well as for families. Seated in sleds, the adults and children in Photo 3.4 are sitting upright in very close proximity to one another. Some hold the sled; others hold each other. Most of the sledders focus their gaze forward to the given/real lower left corner of the frame, connoting in this visual

Photo 3.4 Family holidays in Estonia (http://www.visitestonia.com/en/things-to-see-do/estonia-for-people-like-you/families-kids, accessed 7/11/09)

Photo 3.5 Estonian folklore (http://www.visitestonia.com/en/articles/things-to-see-and-do/history-culture/folklore, accessed 7/11/09)

semiotic the grounding of this activity in tradition and, by extension, in the endurance of the nation.

Photo 3.5 and Photo 3.6 present men and women dressed in native costume, participating in an annual religious ceremony celebrating the

Photo 3.6 Estonian folklore (http://visitestonia.com/en/multimedia/ethnical-series-setu-folk-ensemble-kuldatsauk, accessed 7/11/09)

Setu god of fertility. The woman in Photo 3.5 exhibits a toothy smile with closed eyes, suggesting an emotion of joy as she appears, by the flow of her skirt, to be dancing with the gentleman to her right. The women in Photo 3.6 direct their gaze to the viewer, producing a vector that functions as an image act – a visual image designed to 'do something to the viewer' (Kress & van Leeuwen, 1996: 122). Here, the womens' gaze functions as a visual form of direct address, acknowledging the viewer's presence and participation in the commemoration and maintenance of this tradition and, by extension, of the nation.

Locales

In our (Hallett & Kaplan-Weinger, 2004a) earlier analysis of how the visual semiotic of the Lithuanian tourism website is representative of the construction of an independent identity, we found that 'as Lithuania comes to carry out its independence sociologically as well as politically,... the vast majority of the pictures on the Lithuanian web sites are of places and objects; few include people'. Support for this occurrence is offered by Hummon,

> More often than not, the symbolic landscapes of tourist advertise-ments are peopled with tourists and natives (Table 2). Such is not

always the case: nature land-scapes are frequently unpopulated as a means of symbolically distancing the state from the urban civilization of daily life. (1988: 195)

We note now, that in our more recent analysis of that Lithuanian tourism website, photographs of people are in far greater numbers and no longer in markedly different proportion to pictures of places and artifacts. We can still assert, though, that while the Lithuania tourism website may no longer present 'a self that is more objective than subjective, more factual than emotional, more historical than sociological, more ecologically focused on natural resources than on human resources[, t]he architectures, ecologies, and histories presented are those of longevity, strength, and power, each reflective of a nation that endures as do its buildings, its nature, and its culture' (Hallett & Kaplan-Weinger, 2004a). Today, we can also look at the visual texts of Latvia and Estonia and see that these sites, too, through their inclusion of monuments and nature, present their endurance and vitality.

One of the most salient features of nature, water, is a metaphor of life – like water, life flows through time. Water is both the primary constituent of the human body and the primary nutrient for the preservation of life. In their incorporation of photographs of water, the Baltic tourism websites connote the continued vitality of their nations as they exist today. Images that suggest the movement of the current additionally connote growth and progression – the historicity of the nations as well as their return to their sovereignty. Metaphor, whether presented linguistically or visually, is a communicative device that draws on the human cognitive capacity to connect symbol to meaning. As an 'essential process and product of thought… Metaphor urges us to look beyond the literal, to generate associations and to tap new, different, or deeper levels of meaning' (Feinstein, 1982: 45).

Exemplifying the role of a visual semiotic connoting the vitality and strength of natural resources is the photograph of Estonia's Vanajõe Valley (Photo 3.7). Salient are the high, lush green banks of the river and the blanched rock formations. The river, itself, is barely visible, but its effects are clearly evident in the fertile banks. Between the flourishing greens of the rich foliage along the left bank (the 'given') and the craggy rocky solid cliffs connoting strength on the right bank (the 'new'), the river signals that while nations may change and be changed politically and socially, nature and nationhood can endure. In the context of a stable ecological environment, a nation can capitalize on its once significant

Photo 3.7 Vanajõe Valley (http://www.visitestonia.com/en/multimedia/vanajoe-valley-old-river-valley, accessed 7/11/09)

Photo 3.8 Narva Castle and fortification, Estonia (http://www.visitestonia.com/en/multimedia/narva-castle, accessed 7/11/09)

Photo 3.9 Kumu Art Museum (http://visitestonia.com/en/multimedia/kumu-art-museum, accessed 7/11/09)

Photo 3.10 Vilnius (http://www.lithuaniatourism.co.uk/index.php?id=343)

strength to return to independence and self-reliance sustained and nurtured by both actual and symbolic nutrients.

Images of strength and endurance on tourism websites are not limited to features of the natural environment. As evident in Photo 3.8 of Estonia's Narva Castle and Photo 3.9 of Kumu Art Museum, edifices can construct an identity of both fortitude and vitality as well. Constructed of stone and surviving since the 14th century, the castle and its fortified walls and towers survived numerous attacks. Its existence marks not just survival of the structure, but more importantly for a nation's identity, a secure return to and future in sovereignty.

With a look to the future, the websites of both Lithuania (Photo 3.10) and Estonia (Photo 3.9), through their recent architectural endeavors, also promote modern selves. These glass- and steel-walled structures construct for their respective locales a vision framed in currency and openness. Neighboring structures that reach back into medieval time, these buildings, through their size and shape, construct identities for their nations that are grounded in the future. The steel and glass are at once symbols of reflection and transparency – of nations and governments coming to terms with their pasts and able to show themselves to be prepared to reshape their physical and political identities.

Conclusion

Morley and Robins (1995), in their treatise on shifting national identities in these postmodern times, assert that today's media, including the world wide web, are major forces in identity construction. The media provide nations with a multimodal array of linguistic and visual texts through which to symbolize their identity and, in the process, span traditional political and social boundaries. Additionally, web media allow nations to take up positions that demonstrate rebirth and reconstruction in the context of open and inviting calls to tourists to join in their social action of transformation.

Notes

1. The LSDT is also referred to as the 'Lithuanian Tourist Board' on other websites.
2. Permission to include visual text from the Latvian website was not granted.

Chapter 4

The Tourist as Pilgrim, the Pilgrim as Tourist: Santiago de Compostela

> Even "playful pilgrimages", e.g. trips to Disney World, which, although voluntary rather than compulsory, can assume more serious dimensions when it is realized that they bear many of the hallmarks of civil religion. (Dann, 1996: 78)

In the context of critical discourse analysis, tourism may be seen as social action – an attempt to socially construct and promote a community as significant to both the visitors' and the world's well-being. In addition to the social action inherent in the (re)construction of independent national identities, social action can also take the form of the creation of websites by governmental bodies to promote pilgrimage and tourism to their communities. As these sites entice travelers, they also construct and promote for their communities an identity as a welcoming, soothing setting for spiritual, intellectual and cultural fulfillment.

This chapter, along with Chapters 5 and 6, investigates the construction of pilgrim and tourist identities by the designers of three official websites: one for Santiago de Compostela, Spain, a spiritual capital of Christendom; one for the city of New Orleans, Louisiana, USA, a city rebuilding following a natural disaster; and another for the city of Gary, Indiana, USA, a city trying to revitalize itself in the face of decades of urban blight. The analysis reveals how these cities – through their official websites – have expanded their 'missions' of attracting and comforting 'pilgrims' by stimulating them and others to act as tourists and contribute to the community's economic, political and spiritual growth.

According to tradition, Santiago de Compostela, Spain, is the burial place of the apostle Saint James the Greater, the brother of Saint John the Evangelist (Rudolph, 2004: 3). As the legend goes, James tried, with little success, to evangelize Spain after the death of Christ. When James returned to Jerusalem, he was martyred and his body was left to be devoured by dogs. His disciples removed his remains during the night and placed them in a 'miraculously provided boat' (Rudolph, 2004: 3), which then traveled on its own accord to Northwestern Spain. Rudolph provides the following brief summary of the legend:

> After many trials and miraculous events, the disciples buried the body of James in an old Roman cemetery some distance away from Iria [the capital of Roman Galicia, in northwestern Spain]. There it remained, forgotten and undisturbed for almost eight hundred years, the cemetery having been abandoned and having reverted to a field. However, around 812, strange things began to happen in that field. A mysterious star appeared, and supernatural music was heard by a hermit named Pelayo, who lived nearby. Guided by these signs to the tomb of Saint James (Santiago in Spanish), Pelayo found the body and reported his discovery to the local bishop of Iria. News traveled fast. Soon pilgrims began to arrive at the site of Saint James of the Field of the Star, Santiago de Compostela... A chapel was built over the site, and the bishop moved his episcopal seat to Santiago. (Rudolph, 2004: 4)

Thus, the origins of the modern-day city derive from the legend of Saint James the Greater.

More and more Christians began to make pilgrimages to Santiago de Compostela once word of the miraculous discovery spread. Rudolph (2004: 2) notes, 'Pilgrimage was and is a spiritual exercise in the form of a journey to a place believed to be made holy by a sacred event, or that possesses the relics of a holy person or object'. As Nolan and Nolan (1989: 291) explain, 'Christian pilgrimage in continental Western Europe developed from a desire to be near holy persons who were believed to be especially present on earth in those places where their physical remains were entombed' (see also Brown, 1981). According to Turner and Turner (1978: 6, quoted in Nolan & Nolan, 1989: 12), pilgrimage sites 'are believed to be places where miracles once happened, still happen and may happen again'. In other words, pilgrimage sites are places in which the holy is localized.

Santiago de Compostela gained its greatest fame from medieval pilgrims (Porter & Prince, 2001: 579), for whom Santiago de Compostela was the third most important pilgrimage site after Rome and Jerusalem (Rudolph, 2004; Nolan & Nolan, 1989). The reasons for making the pilgrimage varied from pilgrim to pilgrim, from a penitential require-ment to the search for a miraculous cure (Rudolph, 2004: 5; Nolan & Nolan, 1989: 20). Although it is not clear why Santiago de Compostela became such an important pilgrimage site, some have speculated that one of the reasons for its popularity, at least in the 11th and 12th centuries, was the promotion of the Way of Saint James ('camino de Santiago') by the Cathedral of Santiago (Rudolph, 2004: 3). Nolan and Nolan (1989: 16) provide another possible explanation for its importance: 'Santiago de Compostela is a "classic example" of a shrine that combines touristic importance, pilgrimage festivals, and cultic significance; i.e. it is a religious tourist attraction, a pilgrimage shrine, and a site of a religious festival all in one'. From the very founding of the city, tourism and pilgrimage (arguably a subset of tourism) have played significant roles in the development of Santiago de Compostela. As Cronin explains, this relationship is neither atypical nor ahistorical:

> The pilgrims to Rome, Mecca or Jerusalem are the expression of an ancient link between travel and transcendence. Spiritual quest like the metamorphosis of the hero is the pilgrim's progress from the familiar to the promised land of redemption, illumination, rebirth. (2000: 63)

Multimodal Discourse Analysis: Linguistic Texts

One of the keys to understanding the construction of identity in hypertext is the role language plays. The homepage of www.santiago-turismo.com can be read in multiple languages – Gallego, Spanish, English, Portuguese, French, German and Italian. Each link offers the same information in each language, e.g. each page has the following ten links: The city, Visit Santiago, Accommodation, Santiago for everyone, Basic Services, Way of St. James, Press, Convention Bureau, Film Commission, Tourism quality, Multimedia, Downloads, Links of interest and Contact. Likewise, there is a link with the phrase 'Santiago de Compostela – You'll want more' on most of the links for special tourist offers available through the website. This tourism campaign slogan is salient in how it positions Santiago as a destination not only to fulfill the pilgrimage rite, but also to participate in a number of other experiences including, at this time, a gastronomy tour.

As a holy site, Santiago's sacred origins do maintain a significant presence on the website, but they do so, as the links suggest, alongside more traditional attractions. The site's welcoming message, in providing a balanced presentation of Santiago's religious and secular offerings, clearly speaks to the city's appeal to visitors with a range of interests.

(4.1) **Welcome**
Welcome to Santiago de Compostela. This virtual gateway takes you to the administrative, social and commercial capital of the <u>Autonomous</u>

Community of Galicia; declared a World Heritage City by UNESCO thanks to its multicultural nature and as the final destination of a thousand- year-old pilgrim route: the Way of St. James, which, since the 9th century, has transformed this finis terrae into a meeting place of Western faith and thinking.... The city's visitors will find its treasures exhibited in twelve museums as well as the surprising richness of its contemporary architecture, designed by Eisenman, Hedjuk or Siza, surrounded by Galicia's largest area of parks and gardens.... This setting is alive with cultural expressions – annual music, cinema and theatre festivals, permanent and travelling exhibitions and traditional festivals- organised by the public and private sector, led by the five-hundred-year-old University of Santiago, whose lecture rooms add thirty thousand students to Compostela's stable population of one hundred thousand residents.... These are also joined, throughout the year, by several million visitors. Those who arrive exhausted, motivated by devotion; those who are attracted by the monumental wonders; those who come to participate in language courses or those who choose Compostela as the venue of their professional events: they all end up immersed in the permanent celebration that is the city's life, especially during the Apostle Festival, declared of International Tourist Interest. (santiagoturismo.com/bienvenida/, accessed 23/3/09)

Evidence of Santiago's appeal to historicity in its self-positioning as a sovereign community is present in the second sentence in which Santiago, although recognizing its sacred origins, is now firmly established in the world political, cultural and economic community. Counteracting what may be understood as an identity constructed exclusively of its sacred past, Santiago also promotes its diversity; the city welcomes those travelers 'motivated by devotion' and those motivated by academia, art and festivals.

Introducing the city at the 'Heritage and Culture' link, the website explains,

(4.2) Santiago de Compostela was declared a **World Heritage City** by UNESCO in 1985: "An extraordinary ensemble of distinguished monuments grouped around the tomb of St. James the Greater, the destination of all the roads of Christianity's greatest pilgrimage from the 11th to the 18th century, Santiago de Compostela is beyond the shadow of a doubt one of the world heritage's most obvious properties... an ideal city which is overflowing with history and timelessness as well..." But Santiago de Compostela is also a

European Capital of Culture, a title it was granted in the year 2000 (along with Avignon, Prague, Krakow, Helsinki, Brussels, Bergen, Bologna and Reykjavik) in recognition of its cultural dynamism and its work of cultural dissemination throughout history. A World Heritage City and destination of the Way of St. James, as well as a European City of Culture, Santiago de Compostela is undoubtedly a privileged destination for cultural tourism. (http://santiagoturismo. com/paraTodos/cultural/, accessed 23/3/09)

In the summer, Santiago attracts thousands of travelers who fuel the economy. Understandably, it is not surprising that the city and regional officials would want to encourage travel to Santiago throughout the year. Through its official website, aimed at both religious and secular travelers, Santiago promotes itself as a destination not only for the pilgrim, but also the tourist. Evidence of this promotion for the latter is found in many places throughout the site, including on a link entitled 'Santiago for everyone'. Those aware of Santiago's religious significance will recognize this heading as an implicit, indirect pronouncement of Santiago's appeal to those who hold more than an interest in the sacred. This link intones,

> (4.3) "Santiago for everyone" is thematic Santiago. We compile information corresponding to a specific theme, arranging it according to different motives: culture, business, nature, religion, education, accessible tourism and even cinema. This is the segmentation of Compostela's tourist activities.... We focus on the city's information from these angles and present it with different kinds of public in mind, according to the information they require. It is a vision, a reference, a nod regarding a city that has attractions for all visitors, regardless of their motives. (santiagoturismo.com/paratodos/, accessed 23/3/09)

This appeal to a range of travelers reflects the community's awareness of the need to market Santiago for economic reasons to those who may not have pilgrimage as their sole or even one of their motivations. Rudolph (2004: 34) asserts that pilgrims are not tourists in the more common use of that term. He explains,

> A pilgrim is not a tourist. You have a deeper experience because you are not an observer in the traditional sense of the word... You are part of the cultural landscape, part of the original reason for being and the history of many of the towns through which you pass... This is why the pilgrimage is not a tour, not a vacation, not at all a trip from point A to point B, but a journey that is both an experience and a metaphor rather than an event. (Rudolph, 2004: 34)

Although Santiago's current campaign focuses on attracting the secular tourist as well as the religious pilgrim, it is still possible to characterize Santiago de Compostela tourism as an example of 'religious tourism'. Nolan and Nolan explain the frequency of this phrase among European clergy in the following statement:

> The term [religious tourism] has fewer theological and traditional implications than the word "pilgrim" and encompasses a broader range of motivations for visiting places associated with religious history, art, and devotion. Use of the term also has a kind of neutrality, avoiding implications that pilgrims are somehow better than tourists, for, as shrine administrators sometimes point out, it is entirely possible for a visitor to come as a casual tourist and, because of emotions experienced at the shrine, return for another visit as a pilgrim. (Nolan & Nolan, 1989: 43)

Interestingly, the official Santiago site does not employ the term 'religious tourism', choosing, instead, to maintain the distinction between the two types of visitor. In the attempt to balance, the religious pilgrim is not ignored. The homepage of santiagoturismo.com has as its header a rectangular flash production that includes color pictures advertising accommodations, reservations, activities, theme packages and the telephone number of the 'official reservation office'. However, before these slides begin to scroll, the flash program is initiated with a banner on which a black hand-drawn path emerges from the left bottom corner (the 'given' and 'real' position) of the rectangle and settles about one third into the rectangle. The background color of the flash rectangle is white. On the path appears a male figure, also hand-drawn in black holding and moving along the path with a walking stick. A black hand-drawn church appears in the right corner of the rectangular banner. This same church graphic appears on the right of each banner in the flash headline banner. Between the man on the path and the church, in black block letters appear the words 'There is a reward at the end of The Way', also in a handwritten font (santiagoturismo.com/, accessed 23/3/09). The letters appear somewhat worn as various corners are faded or missing. Obvious reference is made to 'el camino de St. James', 'the road', 'the way'. This banner fades into one that reads 'Compostela – Experience it!' in the same black, worn, font. The somberness of these two slides disappears as the six slides that follow include colored pictures and contemporary black font advertising tourist information. In this series of eight slides, then, the movement from black-and-white to full color, from somber to playful, from religious to secular is displayed and the frame is set for understanding how Santiago's identity is constructed.

Throughout the links on the santiagorurismo.com website, both linguistic and visual texts continue to reinforce the balance of the sacred and the secular. For example, at the 'Celebrations and popular traditions' link, one reads

> (4.4) Although they have lost part of their original functions with the passing of time, Santiago de Compostela's fiestas and traditions are still of great cultural interest; this, along with the city's historical-artistic heritage, is a reflection of its unique personality and character. Compostela's most outstanding fiesta, due to its splendour and international scope, is that of the **Apostle Santiago**, the patron saint of the city, and also of Galicia and Spain. But each fiesta has its own meaning and atmosphere... Thus, although it is to be expected that, in Christendom's third holy city after Jerusalem and Rome, religion would feature prominently in the calendar of feasts **(Christmas, Epiphany, Holy Week, parish feasts)**, the festivities are also related to the earth's productive cycle. This is reflected in the abundance of agricultural and gastronomic festivals **(Magosto, "annual markets"** of the Ascension and the Apostle) or those related to the sun **(San Juan)**. However, their original religious and agricultural nature is now combined with a varied cultural programme: music or dance festivals, street theatre, children's and recreational activities, etc, which enrich and light up the city's traditional celebrations. (santiagoturismo. com/VisitarSantiago/AgendaCultural/Fiestas/fiestas.asp, accessed 23/3/09)

Multimodal Discourse Analysis: Visual Texts

Not all identity construction lies in the linguistic forms of a hypertext. As we have seen, visual text also contributes to the construction of identity through the way it combines and organizes images within and across discourses. Building on Lakoff and Johnson's (1980: 6) theory that 'the human conceptual system is metaphorically structured and defined', this analysis turns now to how the two prevailing metaphors for Santiago – the sacred and the secular – are manifested in the design of the visual texts.

Metaphor, long studied in its linguistic presentation, may also be constructed and interpreted through elements of visual semiotic design. In studying each design, analysts focus on such phenomenon as the right to left and up to down placement of items within a visual space, on the salient positioning of one or more items compared to other items in the same space, and on the juxtaposition of items in the same space. Each of these design elements encodes a message whose interpretation is central to the understanding of the texts as developed by the designer. Visual semioticians focus on these design elements for what and how they contribute to identity construction of both the source and the user.

The following pictures from the Santiago website metaphorically depict the juxtaposition of the sacred and the secular. Further analysis of these visuals demonstrates how, through elements of visual design, the site portrays the sacred as stable, mature and traditional, and the secular as evolving, youthful and modern.

One obvious contrast between Photos 4.1 and 4.2 and Photos 4.3–4.5, rests in color saturation. Photos 4.1 and 4.2 occur together at the 'Cultural' link. In Photo 4.1, the cathedrals on the left side are bathed in soft light.

Photos 4.1 and 4.2 Santiago: heritage and culture

Photo 4.3 Juxtaposing sacred and secular, Santiago (santiagoturismo.com/VisitarSantiago/AgendaCultural/Fiestas/fiestas. asp, accessed 23/3/09)

Photo 4.4 Secular imposed on the sacred, Santiago
(santiagoturismo.com/VisitarSantiago/AgendaCultural/Fiestas/listado
.asp, accessed 23/3/09)

Photo 4.5 Celebrations and traditions, Santiago
(santiagoturismo.com/visitarsantiago/agendacultural/fiestas/particulari
dades.asp, accessed 23/3/09)

The horizon is clouded. No people are visible. The spires reaching to the highest point of 'ideal' in the photo clearly frame a context of somber religiosity. On the right, the bright colors, the futuristic attire and facial cosmetics frame the contemporary secular. Interestingly, both photos are marked with repetition – domes and spires, taller and shorter to the left and an artistically and brightly clad colored image of a woman to the right. Repetition in spoken discourse, according to Tannen (2007), is a technique used to reinforce a message. Here, the meanings that are reinforced are the sacred and the secular. Anchored by the words 'heritage' and 'culture', the photos connote, respectively, the currency of ties to the past and ties to the future. The other contrast, the descriptors, 'World' and 'European', are also significant; Santiago is a part of the larger sacred world. It is also part of the larger European community, but distinct from the non-European community.

A similar balance of the secular and the sacred is apparent in the following visual texts, although not in quite the same array. On the 'Celebrations and popular traditions' link, Photos 4.3–4.5 share a fundamental design layout, but it is a layout that diverges from what visual semiotic theory may predict. With the church placed to the right of each frame and the colorful images to the left, these photos conflict with the 'given'–'new' design. In fact, in these photos, it is the celebratory content that rests in the 'given' position and the church – the anchor of Santiago's sacred identity – that rests in the 'new'. Therefore, to interpret these images, we need to look to different photogenia for an inter-pretative framework. With the colorful festival activities and patrons positioned in the foreground of each photo, the subtle, nondescript tones of the Church in the background suggest the role of the Church and of related religious observance to be the provider of the tradition or foundation for modern celebrations. The Church, and the square outside its doors, provides the cultural, religious and physical environments for the ceremonial observance of the religious festival. As described on the website, one of these festivals, Romeria, is defined in such a way as to encourage appreciation of both its sacred and secular nature.

> (4.5) **Particularitities of our celebrations. Glossary for understand-ing our fiestas: "Romería".** This is a characteristic type of fiesta combining religiosity (mass accompanied by a procession) and secular festivities (open-air dance and snack bars, folklore –bagpipe players and "muiñeira" dances- etc). Those attending "romerías" are called "romeros", who come in search of some kind of favour. They therefore offer the saint a gift or ex-voto, which are normally made of wax and auctioned (to finance the upkeep of the church). This is the case of the **San Lázaro "romería"**, to which people still take pig's trotters, a tradition that has resulted in an exquisite gastronomic recipe that is typically made in the area on the saint's feast day: pig's trotters with cabbage shoots. (santiagoturismo.com/VisitarSantiago/ AgendaCultural/Fiestas/particularidades.asp, accessed 23/3/09)

This analysis of the tourism website of Santiago de Compostela echoes current research in visual semiotics and social constructionism as it contributes to the growing body of tourism writing. As people move through the website, they construct for Santiago and for themselves a tourist and/or a pilgrim identity. This analysis serves as an appropriate introduction to the following two chapters, which also examine the dual role of pilgrim and tourist in increasing economic vibrancy and constructing destination identity for communities searching for revitalization. This is an especially appropriate examination taken in the context of Kaufman's (2001: 63) statement that 'Debate has focused on whether modern mass tourism in the twentieth century is a departure from the traditional act of pilgrimage or its logical extension, a new spiritual search for a sacred center in the modern age'.

Chapter 5

Rebirth of an American City: New Orleans, Louisiana

Introduction

Much as Santiago has been promoted as a site for the non-mutually exclusive functions of tourism and pilgrimage, the official website of the American city of New Orleans, Louisiana, has capitalized on the spiritual in recruiting travelers. New Orleans, in the wake of Hurricane Katrina – one of the most significant natural disasters in the USA in terms of economic cost and human loss – turned to tourism as a way to increase both interest in and monetary flow into their communities. These efforts are not at all surprising in the context of Gilbert's (1999: 280) observation that 'Tourism has played an under-recognized role in the shaping of the modern city as a place to be seen and experienced'.

On the morning of 29 August 2005, a Category 5 hurricane made landfall near the Louisiana–Mississippi state line, and precipitated the flooding of roughly 80% of the city of New Orleans. As one attempt at resurrecting the city, tourism officials in Louisiana have been encouraging people to return to New Orleans in a bid to rebuild much of the devastated city, as well as to drive much-needed tourist dollars back into the state's economy. Famous for its hedonistic celebration of Mardi Gras, New Orleans heavily markets its pre-Lenten celebration largely for economic reasons (see Gotham, 2002). Mardi Gras 2006 differed from previous Mardi Gras celebrations in its need to scale back the event for logistical reasons and, for the first time in the history of the celebration, the call for sponsorship of the events. Clearly, individuals, by partaking not only in tourism and pilgrimage, but also in the wake of Katrina, in restoration and renewal, can serve an important role in the 'rebirth' of this American city.

This analysis, like the previous analysis of the Santiago website, adopts a visual semiotic analytic approach in investigating the construction of a pilgrim/tourist/renewer identity by the official New Orleans, Louisiana and Mardi Gras website designers and promoters. Having roots in pre-Christian traditions, Mardi Gras (literally, 'Fat Tuesday'), the 'last hurrah' before the penitential season of Lent, has become synonymous with the city. Following the devastation of New Orleans by Hurricane Katrina, this analysis focuses on how these sites draw upon specialized texts and images to associate the city and the festival, to characterize a 'self' for tourists and to encourage tourists to participate in the social action of helping in the 'rebirth' of the 'soul' of the city. Through its websites, then, these promoters capitalize on technological advances to mediate the tourist/pilgrim identity within contemporary religious festivity. As such, analytic attention needs to be paid to the use of both linguistic and visual text to activate schema. The Louisiana webpages examined in this chapter make significant use of metaphor in their presentation and, as our thesis argues, in their co-construction of both Louisiana's and the potential traveler's identity.

Metaphor in pre-Katrina Louisiana Tourism Websites

Previously, we discussed how, with relevance to tourism websites, 'The media provide nations with a multimodal array of linguistic and visual texts through which to symbolize their identity and, in the process, span traditional political and social boundaries' in the construction of an 'imagined community' (cf. Anderson, 1991) of locale, residents and visitors (Hallett & Kaplan-Weinger, 2004a: 232). One such body of texts capitalizes on the use of metaphor both in words and images. In perhaps the most profound linguistic-centered work on metaphor, Lakoff and Johnson (1980: 5) define its essence in the following way: '*metaphor is understanding and experiencing one kind of a thing in terms of another*' (original emphasis). Throughout their text, Lakoff and Johnson (1980: 46–47) give specific expressions that are examples of a metaphor, e.g. under the metaphor, IDEAS ARE FOOD, they list 'What he said *left a bad taste in my mouth*', 'I just can't *swallow* that claim', and 'We don't need to *spoon-feed* our students'.

A prominent metaphor found on Louisiana tourism websites before Hurricane Katrina is a similar one – LOUISIANA IS FOOD (see Hallett & Kaplan-Weinger, 2004b). In this metaphor, Louisiana and her cities are dishes to be savored. (All text and photograph data are drawn from www.louisianatravel.com.)

(5.1) *Greater [New Orleans] is a gumbo of experiences* just waiting for you to *pick up the spoon*. Start in the Vieux Carre (the French Quarter) with beignets at the French Market or an authentic jazz brunch at a famous Creole restaurant. Then, *walk off your grillades and grits* on a French Quarter walking tour.

(5.2) Like the *gumbo* for which it is famous, South Louisiana is a rich blend of French, Spanish and African cultures.
(5.3) Like the *gumbo* for which it is famous, South Louisiana is a rich blend. (www.louisianatravel.com, accessed 18/7/04)

(Arguably, this metaphor is more traditionally called a simile as it uses *like*. As Lakoff and Johnson make no distinction between the two, neither do the authors of this chapter.)

Metaphor, long studied in its linguistic presentation, may also be constructed and interpreted through elements of visual semiotic design as the following photos and analysis exemplify. In Photo 5.1, the text 'TASTE Louisiana' appears on the left side of the picture, i.e. the area reserved for given information. On the right, the area in which the new is given, there is a picture of what appears to be a chocho (chayote) stuffed with a type of shrimp salad. The image, integrated with color and texture, contrasts strongly with the block text written in white on a predominantly solid (blank or green) background. As the viewer's eyes move from the more staid presentation of text on the left to the vivid presentation of color and texture on the right, Louisiana as a tourist attraction bursts forth with life and invites those ready to partake.

In Photos 5.2–5.4, the metaphor of LOUISIANA IS FOOD is again found. In each photograph, the word 'Louisiana' is placed next to food to make the equivalence through the collocation, i.e. Louisiana is pecan pie; Louisiana is jambalaya; Louisiana is crawfish. Of particular note here are the types of food that represent Louisiana. The metaphor can be extended to show that Louisiana is sweet (as depicted with the pie), diverse (as are the ingredients in the jambalaya and, previously, the chocho) and spicy (as are the crawfish). In none of these examples is the food bland nor is the food reference about nourishment. Louisiana is crawfish; it is not bread. Like the sensuous food presented as representative of the state's offerings, Louisiana is extolled, by extension, as a locale to be savored rather than merely consumed. Interestingly, in Photos 5.2–5.4, there is

Photo 5.1 Louisiana stuffed choyote (www.louisianatravel.com/where_to_ eat/, accessed 18/7/04)

Photo 5.2 Louisiana pecan pie à la mode (www.louisianatravel.com/, accessed 18/7/04)

Photo 5.3 Louisiana jambalaya (www.louisianatravel.com/, accessed 18/7/04)

Photo 5.4 Louisiana crawfish (www.louisianatravel.com/, accessed 18/7/04)

also a contrast between heat and cold. Louisiana is, therefore, both 'hot', sizzling and exotic, while being 'cool', fresh and contemporary.

Metaphor in pre-Katrina Louisiana Tourism Websites: Reinforcement

Metaphor is typically presented in a lexical or visual context where the relationship between items compared is obvious and direct. At times, however, an utterance or visual design may reinforce rather than state a metaphor and be understood as a non-metaphorical referent that ensures the coherent enactment of identity. Such is the function of the following texts taken from the Louisiana tourism website.

(5.4) This area has a Cajun cowboy feel *with spicy Louisiana cuisine, including great barbeque.*

(5.5) *How to burn off that Crawfish Pie, Jambalaya and Filé Gumbo* in Cajun Country.

(5.6) Of course, wherever you go in Cajun Country, *you can fill up on gumbo, étoufée and corn maquechoux*. And you can buy a gorgeous bowl *to eat it in* from a world champion potter who creates his art right before your eyes.

(5.7) EXPERIENCE EVERYTHING FROM *RED BEANS TO REMOU-LADE* IN GREATER NEW ORLEANS

(5.8) There's a lot *to taste in our gumbo* and a lot to feel in our beat, so step up to our table and put on your dancing shoes. The music's playing!

(5.9) Between the *gumbo* and the magnolias, you'll feel our bass line beating from the banks of the Red River to the crescent of the Mississippi, pulsing with the cadence of the streets and the wall of the blues. (www.louisianatravel.com, accessed 18/7/04)

Metaphor is also reinforced through the use of culinary terms, as seen in (5.10) through (5.13):

(5.10) The small towns surrounding Lafayette offer *a slice* of Cajun life untouched by the fast pace of the city.

(5.11) Here you'll develop *a taste for* jambalaya and for life itself-a joie de vivre-that'll make you want to stay forever.

(5.12) There's always *something cookin'* in Louisiana. Check back often to get the latest news you can use to make your vacation even more enjoyable.

(5.13) What we're *serving up* you just can't find anywhere else, including **mouthwatering recipes** to whet your appetite and **packages** and **coupons** to make getting here for *a taste* all the easier. **Book your trip now.** (www.louisianatravel.com, accessed 18/7/04)

LOUISIANA IS FOOD is not the only metaphor to be found on official Louisiana travel websites. We also find evidence of the metaphor, LOUISIANA IS DIVERSITY. On one level, we see that the dishes shown in the visual texts are diverse in terms of their ingredients. (Perhaps Louisiana is a smaller version of the quintessential American melting pot?) On another level, we notice that specific cultures, such as Cajun, Creole and Native American, are mentioned.

(5.14) There's NOTHING *BLAND* on the menu.

(5.15) This area has a *Cajun* cowboy feel with spicy Louisiana cuisine, including great barbeque.

(5.16) How to burn off that Crawfish Pie, Jambalaya and Filé Gumbo in *Cajun* Country

(5.17) Of course, wherever you go in *Cajun* Country, you can fill up on gumbo, étoufée and corn maquechoux. And you can buy a gorgeous bowl to eat it in from a world champion potter who creates his art right before your eyes.

(5.18) Before the Mayan Temples in South America, before the pyramids in Egypt, before Stonehenge in England, *ancient peoples* built mounds in Louisiana. Here, mounds date back to around 4000 BC, which makes them some of the oldest in the Western Hemisphere. But our *Native Americans* created more than mounds-they influenced the way we eat. We owe the file in our gumbo and the turtle soup served in our fine restaurants to Native Americans. (www.louisianatravel.com, accessed 18/7/04)

In Photos 5.1–5.4, the visual images found on these websites can also convey the linguistically enforced metaphors. Photo 5.5 is a strip of pictures depicting the diverse offerings of Cajun Country. Notice the salience of the food in the second image. The corn and crawfish are the brightest hues of all content in the three photographs; they also compose the only content that fills an entire frame. The crawfish and corn, stacked upon one another, appear, in their abundance, to be falling toward the face of the frame, in a way that reaches out invitingly to the viewer. By contrast, both the water vessel and the woman with the accordion are presented in subtler and less contrastive hues and set back in their respective frames. The vessel seems to ride slowly down the stream toward the 'given' and the 'real' of the natural Louisiana setting, while the woman appears with her head tilted back, eyes closed, and smiling to connote a peaceful enjoyment of the music she plays on her accordion. In this way, the reds and yellow of the crawfish and corn are themselves framed, reinforcing their position as most salient and most exciting of all that Louisiana has to offer.

It is interesting to note that not all Louisiana tourism promoters may be happy with the strong associations that are made between the state and food. A link for a Lafayette, Louisiana, tourism website (http://www.lafayettetravel.com/, accessed 18/7/04) states specifically 'There's

Photo 5.5 Louisiana Cajun scenes (www.louisianatravel.com/regions/cajun.cfm, accessed 18/7/04)

more to Cajun than crawfish'. Apparently, the designers of this website recognize the extensive use of the LOUISIANA IS FOOD metaphor on a neighboring site.

The metaphors LOUISIANA IS FOOD and LOUISIANA IS DIVERSITY may be reacted to, much in the same way as the Lafayette website reacts to the notion that CAJUN IS FOOD. Despite the overall coherence of the metaphor, i.e. the emphasis throughout the website that LOUISIANA IS FOOD, the mere mention of diversity may be an insufficient foundation on which to construct a diverse identity for Louisiana. After all, is the Native American contribution – filé and turtle soup – to the state of Louisiana, described in (5.18), the culmination of Native American cultural influence on Louisiana?

Metaphor in post-Katrina Louisiana Tourism Websites

In contrast to the LOUISIANA IS FOOD metaphors prominent in the period before Hurricane Katrina, the metaphor found on the official Louisiana travel websites following Katrina was LOUISIANA IS A PHOENIX/ LOUISIANA IS REBORN. In fact, soon after Katrina, the word 'rebirth' appeared five times on the first page of the official website for the Louisiana Office of Tourism website (see, for example, Photo 5.6).

The use of the American flag addresses Louisiana's position as one among the 50 states. The physical devastation might be Louisiana's to face, but as part of the USA, they are calling on their nation and its populace for help. The movement suggested by the waves of the flag connotes that Louisiana is alive and active; it has not died, yet still appeals for assistance to recover.

Photo 5.6 Louisiana logo (www.louisianatravel.com/, accessed 27/1/06)

Linguistic text on the website also encourages potential tourists to help Louisiana in her 'rebirth', e.g.

> (5.19) Visiting Louisiana has always been a great idea and now more than ever, Louisiana needs your support. The Rebirth Rewards program is our way of inviting your back. As part of the Rebirth of Louisiana effort, the tourism industry throughout the state has provided offers, discounts and special rates that are available immediately. (www.louisanatravel.com/rebirth_rewards/, accessed 27/1/06)

Visually, the rebirth metaphor is also constructed in photographs.[1] One photograph on the neworleansonline.com website shows a trio of musicians all facing left, but spanning the right half of the frame; the second musician sits at the first musician's right shoulder and the third musician at the second musician's right shoulder. The first musician holds a trumpet to his mouth. The second musician's face and instrument are shielded by the first musician's body. The third has a brass mouthpiece to his lips; the rest of the instrument is obstructed. His gaze is directed downward as if note-reading. Above the head of this musician is the reflection of a light in a mirror. In the relative darkness of the photograph, this light is quite salient. The viewers' gaze is drawn to this light – a light that may metaphorically signify rebirth and renewal. Because of the musicians' left-directed stance, the music seems to flow to the left, connoting an anchoring of New Orleans' musical culture in pre-Katrina's stable past. The dominant image of the light in the top, right quadrant, in turn, connotes that New Orleans seeks a new light in the form of energy that must return to the city for the sake of the city and its populace. The text in this photograph reads 'Welcome Back to New Orleans', ambiguous or polysemous in welcoming back the city of New Orleans to its pre-Katrina conditions, the people of New Orleans who fled the disaster and/or the tourists this campaign is meant to draw.

The furling American flag is adopted in another photograph on the neworleansonline.com site, where it serves as an anchor of the plea and position New Orleans takes as part of its campaign for 'rebirth'. Grounded in the image of a furling American flag, city landmarks, including St. Louis Cathedral, are presented as covered by the flag, suggesting New Orleans' appeal to their nation for protection and sustenance. New Orleans is positioned as a part of America; citizens of New Orleans are Americans and Americans are part of New Orleans. In the furthest left third of the photograph, the flag is opaque; its darkness and brightness connote the strength and vibrancy of America as it sheds its vigor upon the battered region. Moving to the right, to the reality of the present, New Orleans finds itself cast in the transparency of the flag. Its needs, too, are transparent. The stars and stripes, the power and vitality, of the USA must reach out to aid New Orleans. The call to social action, the participation in tourism and pilgrimage, the attendance at Mardi Gras, is a patriotic deed – more than a social action, more than a religious observance; it is an appeal to join a community, to share in celebrating a city and a lifestyle and to participate reflexively in the (re)construction of a city and a self.

A logo that appeared early in 2006 attempts to attract tourists (back) to New Orleans by incorporating the Mardi Gras theme and by drawing on the pre-Katrina theme of 'open all year'. However, post-Katrina, that theme is capitalized on to address the serious economic needs of the community in order to rebuild its infrastructure. 'New Orleans' is presented in uppercase, uneven, playful font sitting above the informally written phrase 'happenin' every day' which, itself, is presented in six times smaller, lowercase font. The second 'N' in 'New Orleans' shares its right-most stroke with the stick handle of a Mardi Gras mask, the kind a reveler might wear when participating in the festivities. The logo pays tribute, through the inclusion of the mask, to the city's Mardi Gras identity, and, in the process, reinforces the message that New Orleans continues to function as a destination for tourists. Post-Katrina marketing continues to appeal to the city's relaxing, celebratory, party atmosphere, even exploiting informal register – 'happenin' every day' – to mark the community's easy-going stance in the wake of the hurricane's destructiveness. A post-Katrina pilgrimage to New Orleans is more than a pre-Lenten celebration; it is a response to a call for social action initiated by the hurricane's destructiveness as well as by appeals such as the following:

> (5.20) Many of you have asked how you can help New Orleans. First, visit New Orleans, a city that annually welcomes 10 million visitors. Stay in our hotels and eat in our great restaurants. Visit our museums, Harrah's Casino, music clubs and art galleries. Shop along Royal and Magazine Streets. In doing this, you will help bring back this city's top industry: tourism. (www.neworleansonline.com/ rebuilding/help.html, accessed 27/1/06)

Three years after Katrina, the New Orleans and Louisiana websites have lessened their focus on the need to renew and rebuild the area. The current New Orleans logo features a gold fleur-de-lis on a brown background (Photo 5.7). Connoting Louisiana's French heritage, the

Photo 5.7 New Orleans logo (http://www.neworleanscvb.com/, accessed 7/11/09)

fleur-de-lis became the state symbol in 2008. Its position on the left side of the logo, to the left of the words 'New Orleans', anchors the state and the city in the stability of the given – a new way to envision the rebirth of the physical and social community.

This repositioning of the city is explained in an e-mail we received from Nathan Williams, Interactive Director for the New Orleans Tourism Marketing Corporation. He informs us that

> our New Orleans perception research (which we performed quarterly after the storm for perhaps two years) did not support a patriotic theme for future advertising. Unlike New York city in the aftermath of 9/11 where people were greatly stirred by patriotic messages, people were not inclined to show interest in visitation through this type of imagery. The Rebirth logo was used in 2006, but was then replaced with another shared brand mark in 2007, Forever New Orleans, which is still in use today.

Before Hurricane Katrina hit New Orleans, the websites that promoted Louisiana and New Orleans tourism called tourists to (quite literally) partake in what their communities offered. Following Katrina, the websites presented a twofold call to social action: one to enjoy all the pleasures (akin to Mardi Gras) and another to participate in the resurrection of a city (akin to the Lenten season). Most recently, Katrina is referenced quite minimally on the websites. For example, present on the New Orleans Convention and Visitors Bureau website (nomcvb.com) is a link creatively labeled 'voluntourism' – offering a combined experience for the traveler. Accessing this link, one finds

> (5.21) Since Hurricane Katrina and its aftermath, the metropolitan New Orleans community has been the beneficiary of an incredible outpouring of support from visitors to New Orleans. From convention visitors to leisure travelers, church groups to high school and

college students, people have shown incredible generosity in giving of their time and talent, and a great deal of elbow grease, helping the city of New Orleans in its recovery and restoration. (http://www. neworleanscvb.com/static/index.cfm/contentID/745/sectionID/1/ subsectionID/745, accessed 7/11/09)

Presented along with this invitation and greatly maximized in comparison with it, is additional textual evidence of New Orleans' return to its pre-Katrina identity as a tourist locale. In a series of flash photographs on the main page of the website, one finds the following images, each promoting a seminal reason for visiting the city (Photos 5.8–5.10).

Photo 5.8 Mardi Gras (http://www.neworleanscvb.com/static/index.cfm/ contentID/363/sectionID/1/subsectionID/0, accessed 7/11/09)

Photo 5.9 Nightlife (http://www.neworleanscvb.com/listings/index.cfm/ catID/18/sectionID/1/subsectionID/582, accessed 7/11/09)

Photo 5.10 Gaming (http://www.neworleanscvb.com/static/index.cfm/
contentID/583/sectionID/1/subsectionID/583, accessed 7/11/09)

Conclusion

Commenting on Aristotle's claims in his *Rhetoric*, Mahon (1999: 75)
writes, 'People are attracted to metaphors precisely because they learn
new things from them, seeing connections where previously they had not
seen any. Metaphors bring things vividly "before the eyes" of listeners or
readers, and the pleasing mental effort required to understand them
makes them memorable'. For texts like the pre- and post-Katrina sites
examined above, metaphor plays a seminal role in not only recontextualizing a community as a phoenix rising, but also a potential tourist as the
morning sun.

Note

1. Permission to publish the two photographs and single logo described was not
   granted.

Chapter 6

'100 Years... Steel Strong': Forging an Identity for Gary, Indiana

Introduction

The official website of the city of Gary, Indiana (USA) and the related links, similar to the previously analyzed sites for Santiago and New Orleans, can be analyzed in terms of how content and design construct an identity for the city and function to promote social action. In the case of Gary, a historic steel town that has lost over 60,000 inhabitants in the last 50 years and has been characterized by native-born Nobel Laureate Joseph Stiglitz (nobelprize.org) for how 'the poverty, the discrimination, the episodic unemployment could not but strike an inquiring youngster', this social action revolves around persuading individuals to recognize the city for more than its industrial identity.

Johnstone (2002: 223) states, 'Discourse analysts have found the idea of performance useful in understanding how aspects of personal identity such as gender, ethnicity, and regional identification are connected to discourse'. Just as individuals perform a self, so can places. Throughout this text, we illustrate how official government websites capitalize on processes of identity construction explored by Wodak *et al.* (1999) and Hall (1996) to promote their communities to potential tourists. We also illustrate how multimodal discourse analysis, in incorporating both visual semiotic and critical discourse analysis, offers researchers a range of texts on which to conduct the study of identity construction. Using both visual and linguistic texts as data, this chapter, like Chapter 5, focuses on how a unique regional or social identity may be constructed through, among other things, the use of metaphor. However, in contrast to the use of metaphor in the call to social action to rebuild a community devastated by a natural disaster, this chapter explores a call to social action to aid in the regeneration of a community suffering the devastation of economic distress.

The city of Gary and its professional sports teams, the Gary SouthShore RailCats baseball team (whose mascot shoulders a steel beam as a baseball bat) and the Continental Basketball Association's

Gary Steelheads (whose mascot is a large Great Lakes steelhead fish named 'Steelie'), use steel metaphors and linguistic ambiguity to present and construct a community's identity that is at once proud of its 'rich history' while 'preparing to be a technological superpower' (www.gary.in.us/visit_hist.asp, accessed 4/4/06).

Founded in 1906 by Elbert H. Gary, an attorney for US Steel, the city of Gary is, according to www.gary.in.us/visit_hist.asp (accessed 4/4/06), 'an industrial city built around a booming steel industry'. As Gary celebrated its centennial in 2006, the official centennial website explained that

> (6.1) The Celebration allows an opportunity to build new bridges and mend old fences: geographically, economically, racially, and generationally. The celebration's planning invites everyone to participate and encourages new commitments to promoting civic pride. The intended result will be a community of prouder-than-ever citizens, more knowledgeable about Gary's history and more enthusiastic about the City's future. (www.garycentennial.com/welcome.asp, accessed 8/4/06)

Despite the centennial organizers' hopes, the city of Gary has a huge image problem to overcome. In his book, *The Worst Towns in the U.S.A.*, Crow introduces the section on Gary in the following manner:

> We think it's sad to be so predictable, but this journal of discovery would lose all credibility if it did not include Gary, Indiana. Its listing here is required for all sorts of reasons – but most importantly because it is a benchmark against which all the other places we've picked can be judged. After all, by including Gary, we're making lots of other rotten places look good by comparison!... The town's infamy has spread worldwide, so that whispering "Gary, Indiana" is like invoking the bogeyman to frighten naughty children into quiet submission. (Crow, 2005: 84)

After describing Gary as a 'hell hole', Crow (2005: 86) ends the section on Gary with the following: 'Surely there must be SOME good news? Well, according to one travel guide, "five interstates slice their way through Indiana, providing a swift but boring means of getting in, through and out of the place as quickly as possible"'. Such commentary is not new in Gary's history. Lane provides the following quote in an issue of *Steel Shavings*:

> In January 1929, a 23-year-old former *Post-Tribune* reporter named Arthur Shumway published a biting satire about Gary's culture, or

lack of it, in the magazine *American Parade*. Entitled "Gary, Shrine of the Steel God: The City That Has Everything, and at the Same Time Has Nothing," it asserted: "Gary, whatever else, is a paradox. It is busy; it is dull. It is modern; it is backward. It is clean; it is filthy. It is rich; it is poor. It has beautiful homes; it has sordid hovels. It is a typical overgrown mill-town; it is a unique new city of the old world. It has a past, but it has no traditions. It has a feeble glow of culture, yet the darkness of prehistoric ignorance." (2006: 88)

Clearly, the city of Gary still has much to do (and has had much to do for a long period of time) to improve its image, let alone promote tourism.

Steel as Metaphor

Using Lakoff and Johnson's (1980) notion of metaphor, we map the metaphor found throughout the Gary city websites as GARY, INDIANA IS STEEL and extend the metaphor to include STEEL IS STRENGTH and, by logical extension, GARY IS STRONG. As defined in the call for papers for the 2006 conference 'Steel Cities: Tradition, Transition and Transformation', steel is 'both a fundamental, functional, interior fabric and a symbolic, highly visible substance [that] permeates the structures, flows, practices and narratives of contemporary tourism' (www.tourism-culture.com, accessed 30/6/06).

When a website for a city is constructed to incorporate this metaphor, its goal is to help potential tourists (re)conceptualize that city. The metaphor GARY IS STEEL, which is an oft-used metaphor for Gary as evidenced by the above quote from Shumway, presents a relationship, according to Kövecses (2002), of target to source. Gary, the target, takes on characteristics of steel, the source. As a source, steel can be said to be mapped onto Gary. In turn, steel functions as the target for another source, strength. Through extension, then, strength, and every other source mapped onto steel, is cognitively mapped onto Gary by those who come in contact with the GARY AS A STEEL CITY metaphor.

Throughout the website for the city of Gary, we find numerous examples of the role steel has played and continues to play in forming an identity for this city. Indeed, our analysis of the official website for Gary and its related links reveals that the city and steel are often synonymous. We consider, for example, the following statement about the city's founding on the main website:

(6.2) One thing Gary is full of is Culture and History. Founded in 1906 by Elbert H. Gary, an attorney for US Steel, Gary is writing its next chapter in history. Historically, Gary is an industrial city built around a booming steel industry. Times are changing, though. Gary is preparing to be a technological superpower, but our rich history will never be forgotten. (www.gary.in.us/visit_hist.asp, accessed 4/4/06)

This theme is echoed in the official logo of the Gary centennial that is found not only on the centennial website, but also on the cover of a special volume of *Steel Shavings* entitled *Gary's First Hundred Years* (Photo 6.1).

In the center of the logo, we see molten steel being poured over the Earth, connoting Gary's role in bringing the strength of steel to the world. Surrounding this image, we see the slogan 'City of the Century', which promotes Gary's 100 years of existence as well as its featured role in the current century. Once again, we see, in the adjacent positioning of the text and the image, the synonymy of Gary and steel reinforcing the metaphor of GARY IS STEEL.

The Gary centennial website further reinforces the metaphor of GARY IS STEEL by including steel not only in the logo, but also the word 'steel' in

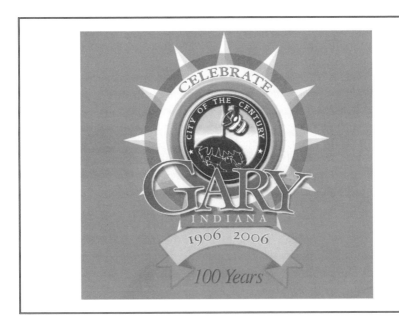

Photo 6.1 Gary centennial logo (www.garycentennial.com/, accessed 8/4/06)

Photo 6.2 Gary centennial banner (www.garycentennial.com/, accessed 8/4/06)

a linguistic word play in the site's banner. In this case, the banner reads '100 Years…Steel Strong' with a play on the minimal pair 'still' and 'steel'. This tells us Gary is not only as strong as steel, steel-strong, but also <u>still</u> strong (Photo 6.2).

In another attempt to revitalize the economically depressed city of Gary, instill civic pride and attract tourism, the local government has developed two professional sports teams: a minor league baseball team and a basketball team. Interestingly, both teams continue to map the steel metaphor onto Gary. The Gary SouthShore RailCats began minor league play in May 2003 in a stadium built with United States Steel Corporation. One of the stated community goals of the organization, as it creates new capital for Gary through tourism, is 'to fund and promote youth baseball and softball programs' (www.railcatsbaseball.com/Press Release_detail.asp?ID = 375, accessed 8/4/06).

The metaphor of GARY IS STEEL is reinforced in the name of the RailCats' stadium, i.e. US Steel steel yard (Photo 6.3). The steel mill and the stadium are close both in terms of physical location and in metaphor; the ballpark is literally right across the street from the steel mill. Photo 6.4 shows how the smoke and steam from US Steel is visible from the ballpark.

The GARY IS STEEL metaphor is also found in the logo for the stadium, as seen in Photo 6.5, taken from the cover of a game day program. Several elements comprise the logo: a cat claw (from the RailCat mascot) holding a baseball on which the letters 'USS' (for United States Steel) appear and the words 'STEEL YARD', 'UNITED STATES STEEL', 'GARY, INDIANA' and a banner stating 'HOME OF THE RAILCATS' all superimposed over the home plate. What is most interesting in this logo is the fact that the capital letters in 'STEEL YARD' appear to be made of steel, as evidenced by the rivets in each letter. Not only does the word 'STEEL' appear twice

Photo 6.3 US Steel steel yard, Gary (llnw.image.cbslocal.com/27/2008/04/09/175x131/WBBM0409garyrailcats.jpg, accessed 9/4/08)

(three times if we consider what the last 'S' in 'USS' stands for), but the imagery of steel also appears in the logo. The uppercase font used in the text is itself an anchor of strength and power as well.

The railcat image is also part of the visual texts in Photos 6.6 and 6.7 As a source domain, the railcat, its teeth and its claws map metaphorical meaning onto the baseball team, and, in conjunction, onto the city of Gary. Cats are agile and quick, fierce and stealthy. Mascots are common, but what is unusual is this mascot's use of steel (an i-beam) instead of a baseball bat, lending again to the metaphor that Gary and all things Gary are steel strong.

The GARY IS STEEL metaphor is even more prevalent on the websites for the basketball team. In 2006, Gary is referred to as 'steel city' on the very first page of the team's website:

> (6.3) Located in downtown Gary, the Genesis Convention Center is just 35 minutes from Chicago's Loop. It is part of the re-birth of the Steel City's downtown area as a major sports and entertainment venue and has easy access from the Indiana Toll Road or I-80/94. This makes the arena easily reachable from anywhere in Northwest Indiana and the Chicagoland area. (www.steelheadshoops.com/genesis/history/, accessed 8/4/06)

Photo 6.4 US Steel steel yard with smoke from US Steel (Gary © Rick Hallett)

Gary's basketball team is known as the Gary Steelheads. As the mascot of the RailCats reinforces the steel metaphor, we find even stronger reinforcement of the metaphor in text and images that promote the basketball team. Photo 6.8 shows the appearance of the team logo in 2006. The logo shows a grey fish, 'Steelie', outlined and detailed in blue and black; the team name is presented in the same shade of blue and in block letters outlined in black. This symmetry of color as well as the power and toughness implied by the fish's snarling facial expression and clenched fist unifies the mascot to the font – suggesting the team itself, and by extension, the city of Gary itself, is strong. Indeed, the steelhead is anthropomorphized, thus connecting the human fan to the superhuman-like steelhead. With Steelie's gaze focused to the right of the frame, the future of both the team and its city is implied. In the logo, Steelie is placed within a basketball hoop and net, suggesting either (if the fish is emerging out of the top of the net) the rise of the team and its city or (if the fish is

Photo 6.5 RailCats scorecard (personal collection)

Photo 6.6 SouthShore RailCats logo www.railcatsbaseball.com/excellence/
missionstatement/ (accessed 26/2/09)

Photo 6.7 US Steel steel yard banner, Gary (www.railcatsbaseball.com, accessed 26/2/09)

Photo 6.8 Gary Steelheads mascot (original) (en.wikipedia.org/wiki/File: Steelheads_Logo.jpg, accessed 4/5/06)

descending as does a basketball into the net) the success (it is 'scoring') of the team and its city. With either interpretation, the association between the team and its city is clear – they are mutually strong, mutually focused on winning and on progress.

Photo 6.9 depicts the logo that appears on the Steelheads website as of May 2008. This new logo has the Steelheads name placed above the fish in ideal position. Additionally, the name is written in a sweeping uppercase squared font and underlined to indicate both prominence/dominance

Photo 6.9 Gary Steelheads mascot (current) (www.steelheadshoops.com/, accessed 13/5/08)

and movement. 'Gary' is found in uppercase font as well, placed just above the 'Steelhead' name, but in a much smaller size. The city, then, does not exist prominently in this logo; although Gary is placed in a higher and more ideal position, its size suggests the city itself is not as salient as the team. Movement is also connoted in the motion of the fish, seemingly jumping out of water, mouth open, teeth showing to imply a sense of an impending bite, as if the steelheads were closing in on prey – i.e. the opposing team. The blue swirl that surrounds the front of the steelhead, as well as the basketball that sits just above it, reinforces the context of movement.

Perhaps even more impressive than his physical appearance, is Steelie's personal history, which is found on the Steelheads' website. Here, he offers his personal narrative:

> (6.4) I was born on Feb. 18, 2000 – the same day the Steelheads' basketball team was born. I started my life as a little guppy in a stream, but like all steelheads, I headed to the Great Lakes and Lake Michigan. Yes, I was a little guy in the Marquette Park Lagoon and worked my way over to Marquette Beach. Now I reside in the Genesis Center, but I am very migratory. You see me all over the Calumet Region whether it is at parades, festivals or birthday parties. I even go out on boats, but not to fish. (www.steelheadshoops.com/ genesis/history/, accessed 8/4/06)

He continues,

> (6.5) I am in every nook and cranny in the arena. I may come sit down with you for awhile. You know I love the fans because you are so friendly to me and the whole organization knows just how very important you are to our team. I may be leading the cheers with the Steelhearts, our great cheer and dance squad. I even help out with the pre-game introduction of our Steelheads. (www.steel headshoops.com/genesis/history/, accessed 8/4/06)

As a mascot, Steelie interacts with the crowd. The team is not his or yours; it is 'ours'. Yet Steelie is the personification of the team, even more anthropomorphized by his use of his own voice and in his interest in interacting with the fans.

Attention must also be given to the name of the Steelheads' cheerleading squad. The compound noun 'Steelhearts' connotes a mixture of toughness and sensitivity. The 'heads' of the team are the players – those who engage in competition and focus on winning. The 'hearts' of the team are the cheerleaders – those who are responsible for emotionally engaging the fans in appreciation of the team and its pursuits. Together, 'heads' and 'hearts' complete the anthropomorphized mascot and logo; they present the team and the city of Gary in balanced pursuit of the minds and emotions of its current and prospective fans.

The linguistic and visual texts on these websites succeed as metaphors; steel is mapped onto Gary; strength is mapped onto steel; and, therefore, strength is mapped onto Gary. This strength, though, is not a 'dull', 'backward', 'filthy', 'poor' strength as Shumway might label it. It is instead a strength marked in legacy, in black and white – a strength like that constructed in Photo 6.10 where the pouring molten steel is juxtaposed with and compared to Gary. The message is connoted – Gary is resilience. Gary endures. In Wodak et al.'s terms, Gary dwells in the contemporary, but owes that existence to its historicity. The community and its ballplayers, citizens and steelworkers, demonstrate the vigor, power and vitality that demonstrate and work to retain renewal.

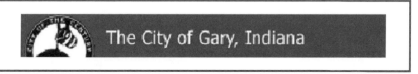

Photo 6.10 Homepage banner (www.gary.in.us/visit_hist.asp, accessed 13/5/08)

Conclusion

Analysis of the travel websites for Santiago, New Orleans and Gary reflects the nascent position of the world wide web as a mediator of tourism. Santiago de Compostela's site constructs potential religious pilgrims as tourists as well. In turn, the Louisiana and Gary sites construct potential tourists as revivers. The life that will be metaphorically breathed into these cities through their respective websites will lead not only to increased tourism, but also to increased promotion and improved financial standing. The world wide web continues to develop as an ideological mediator of tourism. As they move through the hypertext – linguistic and visual – that marks the web construct, web users participate in the co-constructional process of identity formation. These websites call upon their users to participate in an ideological dialectic that results in the construction of each of the cities as an 'imagined community' and of the web visitors as 'tourists' and 'restorers'.

Chapter 7

The Tourist as Patriot: Sports and Nationalism

Introduction

This chapter explores the sports Hall of Fame as a tourist destination, concentrating on how such halls are constructed through linguistic and visual texts to draw both the attendance and the currency of the tourist. Additionally, in the context of Chapter 4 and the positioning through its official website of Santiago de Compostela as a destination for both tourism and pilgrimage, we argue that the websites of these Halls of Fame serve similarly to honor the achievements of individuals, the endeavors in which they involve themselves, and the places in which and the tools with which these achievements are realized.

Sports activities – whether professional or amateur, organized or spontaneous – occupy a unique position in the USA. Participated in by all age and both gender groups, sports like baseball, basketball, football, soccer and golf, at the professional and amateur levels, grab the attention of players and observers alike. In fact, 'Participation in organized sports has become a common rite of childhood in the United States' (www.fitness.gov/activity/activity4/youthsports.pdf, accessed 6/7/08). In their analysis of the role of sports in American culture, Washington and Karen (2001: 87) note that, 'sports, indeed, constitute a major part of the US economy: the expenditures in 1998 for commercial sports totaled $17.7 billion and an additional $21.4 billion was spent on physical fitness, golf, bowling, and sports and recreation clubs' (US Census Bureau, 1999: 46). They explain that

> The pervasive interest in sports is revealed in varied forms. Sports get a separate section in every major daily newspaper; they fill stadiums and arenas around the world on a regular basis as people root, often maniacally, for their home teams; they spawned thousands of rotisserie leagues (i.e., sports leagues composed of fan-chosen teams) along with debates about the best players, teams, etc.; they occupy the weekends and evenings of parents and children; they receive massive expenditures of funds by schools and colleges in

the United States; they occupy hours and hours of weekly commercial radio and television air time with accompanying astronomical advertising revenues; and they are increasingly the object of public policy as they engage the concerns of voters and politicians at the local, state, and federal levels. (Washington & Karen, 2001: 187–188)

Schmitt and Leonard echo this perception of the pervasive role of sports in American society as they explain,

> Formal sport acts are frequently described in the media. Professional and collegiate happenings are televised and retelevised (as in instant replay) [and cable sports channels that show replays of entire games], broadcast and rebroadcast. Outcomes of such events are reported and scrutinized in newspapers and sports magazines and discussed on television and radio. Interviews with players, coaches, owners, and fans appear in multitudinous media forms. Sports pages attend to local as well as national and international events. High school newspapers and yearbooks highlight players and records. Informal sport acts and their participants, too, are affected by the mass media even though they are infrequently depicted in them. (Schmitt & Leonard, 1986: 1092–1093)

The result of this pervasiveness is the creation of heroes and icons – individuals and teams the public wishes to see and even, for some, to be. As icons, athletes can be immortalized and this can be accomplished not only through memories and photographs that fans may hold on to, but also through formal organizations like Halls of Fame that enshrine these heroes and provide a place for their accomplishments to be honored. When we visit these Halls and when we participate in honoring our heroes, we contribute further to their social construction and maintenance as icons. In the process, echoing Carbaugh's (1996) social constructionist model, we demonstrate our position as knowledgeable, dedicated, appreciative fans of the game and of its players. According to Schmitt and Leonard (1986: 1096), sports Halls of Fame 'involve a commemorative quality. The Baseball Hall of Fame, the National Football Hall of Fame, and the Basketball Hall of Fame encourage fans to eulogize and remember the greats of yesterday. These "collective monuments," as we label them, commemorate a group of athletes who have reached the apex of success in the same sport'.

Schmitt and Leonard (1986: 1088) explain that Halls of Fame provide a place for the 'postself', which they define as *'the concern of a person with the presentation of his or her self in history;. . .* the postself is a role-identity, albeit one that concerns the very essence or permanence of selfhood'. Halls of Fame, as well as other forms of remembrance, are part of a larger text that 'facilitate[s] the postself by providing occasions, settings, and processes though which its participants can be remembered, eulogized, and endeared' (Schmitt & Leonard, 1986: 1088).

With the unique connection between sports teams and sports fans in the USA and other locales, vacations to sports Halls of Fame become very much like pilgrimages. Athletes are heroes and, at times to some fans, icons with as much (might we say for some, even more) iconic significance as religious figures. In the context of social constructionism, the opportunity to view and interact with the memorabilia of the icon is an opportunity to share in the life, exploits and triumphs of that icon. In the framework of Carbaugh's social constructionist model, we may, as Hall of Fame visitors, demonstrate who we are by the way we participate in our expedition. As Schmitt and Leonard (p. 1098) explain,

> athletes are not the only ones who are immortalized for participating in memorable athletic performances. The fame or discredit that accrues to them may extend to their families and friends, to other aspects of the sport act, and, probably, to some of their fans. This expansiveness occurs largely because the anchoring of activity to its environing world is complex and paradoxical.

In a previous analysis of the US Pro Football and Soccer Halls of Fame websites, respectively, we examined the function of these texts not only in the self-promotion of the sports, but also in terms of their role in the social construction of a sport's and its fan identities. Our findings demonstrate how these sites 'incorporate linguistic and visual text in the discursive construction as ideological shrines of the physical places they represent; the sites can be seen in a critical discourse analytic perspective as enticing sports enthusiasts to undertake a pilgrimage to a holy memorial to the individuals, teams, and events they revere' (Hallett & Kaplan-Weinger, 2008). This chapter, while similarly focusing on the role of Halls of Fame as hallowed ground and on the use of linguistic and visual texts in the construction of this identity, considers an additional component of tourism as pilgrimage – in the context of visiting the Baseball Hall of Fame and to a significant but lesser extent the Basketball Hall of Fame – the opportunity to create, express and encourage a patriotic self.

Baseball Hall of Fame: Mission, Promotion and History

Internationally, baseball and softball are actively participated in. Data from Little League Online reveal that in 2006, 2,664,540 children participated in teams organized by their association (www.littleleague.org/media/06participation.asp, accessed 14/7/08). Millions of children play in leagues sponsored by schools, park districts and private organizations. In the USA, 'Although sports are not viewed as a panacea for society's ills, sports participation that emphasizes skill-building and socially acceptable responses to personal relations has proven to be a popular aid in the education of youth' (www.fitness.gov/activity/activity4/youthsports.pdf, accessed 10/7/08). The history of baseball and its place in American society is promulgated with its origins recognized in the following way:

(7.1) The first scheme for playing baseball, according to the best evidence obtainable to date, was devised by Abner Doubleday at Cooperstown, N.Y. in 1839. (www.baseballhalloffame.org/museum/history.jsp, accessed 19/7/08)

Today, Cooperstown, NY, is the home of the first sports Halls of Fame – the Baseball Hall of Fame. Noting the game's association to the USA, the Hall presents its mission as being

(7.2) dedicated to fostering an appreciation of the historical development of the game and its impact on our culture by collecting, preserving, exhibiting and interpreting its collections for a global audience, as well as honoring those who have made outstanding contributions to our [the US's] National Pastime. (www.baseballhalloffame.org/museum/mission.jsp, accessed 19/7/08)

The National Baseball Hall of Fame is promoted on its website's homepage as 'Preserving History • Honoring Excellence • Connecting Generations' (www.baseballhalloffame.org/index.jsp). This petition across the ages, structured in the progressive tense, places the Baseball Hall and the sport of baseball itself in the role of an ongoing 'great showcase' of a heritage that spans US geography and the American populace. The Hall of Fame and Museum (www.baseballhalloffame.org/index.jsp) homepage includes among its links 'Sacred Ground exhibit', 'Pride & Passion exhibit' and 'Diamond Dreams exhibit', each of which in name reinforces a religious and/or spiritual metaphor. Additionally, the homepage carries a link 'Baseball as America tour', introduced with the following quote reinforcing baseball's patriotic position in America:

(7.3) I think there are only three things that America will be known for 2,000 years from now when they study this civilization: the Constitution, jazz music and baseball. They're the three most beautifully designed things this culture has ever produced. — Gerald Early, Scholar (http://www.baseballasamerica.org, accessed 19/7/08)

'Baseball, Hot Dogs, Apple Pie, and Chevrolet, They Go Together in the Good Ol' USA'. So intones a popular and iconic commercial jingle of the 1970s. Baseball is America's game. Paying homage to baseball is paying homage to the USA. Paying homage to baseball's greatest players, managers and executives is paying homage to America's heroes. Paying homage to baseball artifacts – its fields, its tools, its prizes – is paying homage to the sacred places and relics of the USA. American poet Walt Whitman explained,

Baseball is the hurrah game of the republic!… That's beautiful: the hurrah game! well — it's our game: that's the chief fact in connection with it: America's game: has the snap, go fling, of the American atmosphere — belongs as much to our institutions, fits into them as significantly, as our constitutions, laws: is just as important in the sum total of our historic life. (http://www.whitmanarchive.org/criticism/disciples/traubel/WWWiC/4/med.00004.77.html, accessed 22/3/09)

Echoing Whitman, author Bruce Catton offers, 'Say this much for big league baseball – it is beyond question the greatest conversation piece ever invented in America' (http://www.baseballtips.com/newsletter/15.html). The Hall's website itself joins in recognizing and promoting the game's role in American life and the Hall's position in constructing and preserving its fans' interests and identity. In 7.4, note the use of 'we' to join the voice of the site with the voice of the tourist.

(7.4) Because baseball has been a part of American culture since the formation of the United States, its fans have always had a special relationship with the game. Because we are curious by nature, and have a thirst to learn more about ourselves and our heritage, we have always had an interest in journeying to Cooperstown. (www.baseballhalloffame.org/news/article.jsp?ymd = 20070221&contentid = 1047&vkey = hof_news, accessed 9/7/08)

The US government also seizes hold of baseball, couching the nation's identity in the game. In a posting on the website of the US Diplomatic Mission to Germany, readers can learn 'About the USA' (http://usa.usembassy.de, accessed 9/7/08) and that 'Baseball Plays to America's

Heart and Mind: (The most American of sports becomes international)'. The site informs the reader that

> It is hard to explain to people from foreign lands, this most American of games; harder still to express its hold on the national soul, the reverential devotion it calls from its fans, and how deeply embedded it is in the very fabric of our national experience. With its broad green fields and slow pace, baseball is firmly rooted in America's pastoral beginnings and often seems untouched by change. (http://usa.u-sembassy.de/etexts/sport/baseball.htm, accessed 9/7/08)

Basketball Hall of Fame: Mission, Promotion and History

Basketball is a similarly popular sports engaged in by children internationally. In the USA, for example, according to USA Basketball, a joint initiative of the US National Collegiate Athletic Association (NCAA) and the National Basketball Association, 'more than 23 million American boys and girls... play basketball' (http://www.usabasket-ball.com/news. php?news_page = 08_youth_basketball_initiative, accessed 15/7/08). The Basketball Hall of Fame addresses its history primarily through its James Naismith Section (http://www.hoophall.-com/ history/bhof-history.html). Credited with inventing the game and its first 13 rules, Naismith,

> (7.5) neither sought publicity nor engaged in self-promotion [but] has had his name attached to the Hall. (www.hoophall.com/history/ naismith-bio.html, accessed 15/7/08)

The mission of the Basketball Hall of Fame, as promoted on its website, parallels that of the Baseball Hall of Fame. With goals to 'enrich and educate' and 'actively involve all fans', the website identifies the Basketball Hall as the 'world's finest sports museum' (http://www.hoo-phall.com/support/bhof-mission.htm). Its history is presented in the context of two members of its Hall of Fame – Julius Erving and George Mikan – and through the voice of someone who seems to be narrating his/her own visit to the Hall. Drawing the website reader/potential Hall visitor into the experience, the author narrates,

> (7.6) "Dr. J was totally awesome," one was saying to a tyke too young to know first-hand. Another was explaining what the red-white-and blue ball of the American Basketball Association meant to the game from 1967 to 1976. I noticed that one member of the original Hall of

Fame Class of 1959, George Mikan, is still around today – a living, 7-foot monument to the very beginnings of the shrine. Speaking of the shrine, this is its third home. The first was at Springfield College, a small, functional facility that offered a fair assortment of artifacts and made almost no effort toward storytelling, which is what helps make the modern Hall so fascinating and fun. The second facility, which served the sport from 1985 to 2002, was far better. It brought interactive displays to the Hall, and created a link between the sports earliest days and its modern era, which made it much more interesting for children. The new Hall of Fame dwarfs both of those facilities in both size and scope. (grfx.cstv.com/photos/schools/bhof/genrel/auto_pdf/newhall3.pdf, accessed 22/3/09)

The history of the Hall, as presented in this narrative, highlights the role of the Hall in not only informing the visitor about basketball, but, even more so, in involving the visitor in the game. The tie to America and patriotism is noted in the coordination between the colors of the ABA ball and the American flag. Historicity is noted, in turn, by the identification of modern basketball as an 'era' having developed from its 'earliest days' and by noting that through storytelling – itself, one of the most interactive of media – the chronicle of the game can be transmitted from generation to generation. Also relevant to the social constructionist experience one can have at the Hall and through the website, is the presence of 'interactive displays', which invite participation in the exhibit and, by extension, in the game and in its players, artifacts and history.

National Baseball Hall of Fame: Linguistic and Visual Analysis

Absorbed by the metaphor of 'baseball as America', the tourist, whether within or outside the USA, may want to learn more, see more about this American icon of recreation. That tourist, wanting to experience the spirit of the game may travel to a ballpark to 'take in a game'. That tourist may also read magazine articles, watch a game on television, listen to a game on the radio or the internet. And that tourist may visit Cooperstown, NY, and the National Baseball Hall of Fame. Founded in 1939 in a city that was the home of Abner Doubleday, believed to be the founder of baseball, the Hall sits in a community that

(7.7) represents a step back in time, with buildings dating to the early 19th century and orange geraniums hanging from classically-styled streetlights. More than 350,000 people travel to the Village each year to pay tribute to our National Pastime by visiting the Hall of Fame, an institution which honors excellence, preserves history and connects generations.... Representing all aspects of Baseball – both on the field and in our culture – the Museum collections total 35,000 three-dimensional artifacts (including bats, balls, gloves, caps, helmets, uniforms, shoes, trophies and awards) and 130,000 baseball cards.... From its embryonic stages, the Baseball Hall of Fame has become an international destination that chronicles the evolution of our National Pastime. From humble beginnings and a small collection of artifacts in the mid-1930s, the Hall of Fame has evolved into a cultural showcase, where people come to learn about the past, and soon discover that Baseball is the common thread of our national spirit. (www.baseballhalloffame.org/about/history.htm, accessed 19/7/08)

Virtual tourists – either those planning a trip to the Hall of Fame or making the web their means of traveling and enjoying the Hall – see this connection between America and baseball reinforced in a number of ways. As the page entitled 'Baseball as Patriotism and Pride: The Connection Between Our National Pastime and the Presidency' offers,

(7.8) The [US] president's annual appearance at the start of each season symbolically renews the bonds that unite the country, its leaders, and the game – a ceremonial springtime rebirth as America's National Pastime. For presidents, baseball offers a welcome connection to a wholesome, all-American image. Baseball and the American presidency have had a long history together. Since baseball's inception in the mid-19th century, Presidents have been involved with the National Pastime in many ways, by participating, watching or supporting. (www.baseballhalloffame.org/history/2004/040330. htm, accessed 19/7/08)

Another link from the Hall of Fame site leads one to an interview with Bill Campbell, 'Former Major League Reliever and Vietnam Veteran'. At the beginning of this interview, the reader learns that

(7.9) Reliever Bill Campbell pitched in his share of pressure situations as an ace reliever during his 15-year major league career. But the pressure he faced on the mound paled in comparison to the life and death danger he faced during his service in the U.S. Army in Vietnam in 1968–1969. (www.baseballhalloffame. org, accessed 19/7/08)

Baseball players. War veterans. The nation's heroes – a singular hero – unite the battle fields of baseball and of war – serving their country on each. Tributes like these function to inform the virtual tourist while also constructing the Hall of Fame's identity as a shrine, the inductee as an icon or idol. The Hall itself is a spiritually fulfilling and patriotic destination. As a website designed to inform potential tourists and sports fans, www.baseballhalloffame.org has much in common with both the US Football and Soccer Halls of Fame, and, as we shall see below, with the Pro Basketball Hall of Fame. In our analysis of the Football and Soccer Hall sites, we concluded that,

> The journey through sports Halls of Fame, then, is a journey not only through the respective games, but also through the legacies of their players in a way that can make the pilgrim at one with the player... Halls of Fame sites offer the patriot/pilgrim a chance to indulge in the spiritual – a chance to adore and revere. (Hallett & Kaplan-Weinger, 2008: 218)

Visually, the Baseball Hall website makes dominant use of a patriotic color scheme – the American flag colors of red, white and blue – to associate itself with the USA and its promoted values, which according to 'Ben's Guide to U.S. Government for Kids' (http://bensguide.gpo.-gov/3-5/symbols/flag.htm, accessed 19/7/08) are

- White: signifies purity and innocence.
- Red: signifies valor and bravery.
- Blue: signifies vigilance, perseverance and justice.

This color scheme is evident in the left side index on the National Baseball Hall of Fame website. Stars, made part of the flag to symbolize the divine heavens and to recognize each state of the Union, are accompanied by one blue and three white stripes, a white baseball with red stitching, and text cast in blue on a white background or white on a blue background. The white stars that also mark each link, turn to red-stitched, white baseballs when the cursor rolls over them (Photo 7.1). In Photo 7.2 on the homepage, a fan dressed in a Hall of Fame jersey holds a membership card framed in red, white and blue, positioned to the right of a ballplayer dressed in a uniform of white and red. The card and, as a result, the act of membership receive salience – they are atop the frame in ideal position and fronted to a degree that distorts their size in relation to the card holder. Accompanied by the directive to 'Become a member!' printed in large blue font and to further one's community with baseball by purchasing a Hall souvenir, both the visual and written texts reach out to the site's viewer to draw him/her into the position of a 'member' of the Hall – just like the heroes enshrined within.

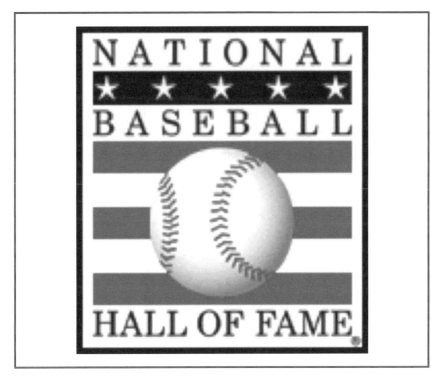

Photo 7.1 Baseball Hall of Fame logo (www.baseballhalloffame.org/, accessed 24/2/09)

A square emblem promoting a Hall of Fame fantasy camp is similarly clad in red, white and blue, stars and stripes, a blue banner, a white and red baseball, all on a white and blue outlined red diamond (base) shape overlapping a blue ribbon, all of which produces in tandem an eight-pointed star (Photo 7.3). 'FANTASY CAMP' is salient in its position atop the lower three levels, the waviness of the banner connoting movement – of a flag, of a banner, of a game – all outside in the brightness of the baseball diamond. For the baseball fan who wants to do more than observe or relive the game, all parts of the game come together, allowing the fan to be player, the dream to be reality, the sacred to be the authentic – simply by participating in six days of play with members of the Hall of Fame – to be a player 'on the same diamond as many greats in baseball history' (http://ww2.baseballhalloffame.com/fantasycamp/, accessed 24/2/09).

In serving to construct the fan identity for the site user, the baseballhalloffame.com site recognizes and encourages input from fans. At

Photo 7.2 Baseball Hall of Fame membership link (shop.mlb.com/shop/index.jsp?categoryId = 2588656&vbID = 0000006, accessed 24/2/09)

the link taking the virtual tourist to the page below, the view is of a virtual tour of a virtual tour. United in the context of baseball fields as 'sacred grounds', are the fields and the fans, the fan dressed in the jersey of a professional ballplayer and (possible) future member of the Hall of Fame. In the bottom left of the text, the fan is in given/real position, seemingly at the controls of what appears on the screen as he 'walks through' a no-longer-existing stadium – itself positioned in the upper right of the screen in new and ideal position. For this fan, the visual text connotes an opportunity to participate in a virtual reality – fan meets sacred ground. His gaze is focused on the display directly in front of him on which he can manipulate the images to the larger screen. The gaze of the website viewer is drawn to the stadium through a vector emanating from the given to new, real to ideal. Photo 7.4 is described as 'A young fan takes a virtual "walk-through" tour of Boston's South End Grounds via a curved 14' × 8' screen'.

Photo 7.3 Baseball Hall of Fame fantasy camp link (ww2.baseballhalloffame.com/fantasycamp/, accessed 24/2/09)

Photo 7.4 Baseball Hall of Fame virtual ballpark tour (www.baseballhalloffame.org/history/2005/05069.htm, accessed July 7/7/08)

Photo 7.5 Baseball Hall of Fame education link banner (education.baseball-halloffame.org/, accessed 24/2/09)

Finally, the educational benefits of the Baseball Hall and the website are promoted, capturing the interest of the school teacher, the student and the historian.

The banner topping the page begins on the reader's/viewer's left with the red, white and blue emblem of the Hall (Photo 7.5). Farthest right is a roughed-up baseball connoting it's been in a game, seen action, experienced the throws and the hits of the heroes who have used it as their tool. Straddling the top middle section of the headline banner are the words 'Enriching Education' in uppercase, white, block letters on a blue face. Through its size and thickness, this font connotes strength compared to the other fonts within this text (Leborg, 2006). As the text below it in cursive font connotes, the Hall acknowledges its mission to unite fans of all ages by providing a place where they can gather to recall, relive or experience, initially, the contributions made by baseball. By 'preserving history, honoring excellence, and connecting generations', the Hall is homage to American culture as much as it is a storehouse of baseball memorabilia.

Naismith Basketball Hall of Fame: Linguistic and Visual Analysis

In comparison to the Baseball Hall of Fame website, the Basketball Hall site incorporates far fewer references to patriotism and pilgrimage. Baseball is America's game; basketball is just one of a number of sports played in America. Nonetheless, a few such references can be found. For example, along with the Basketball Hall's mission to preserve the sport's history and heroes, it also promotes its educational mission:

(7.10) **Educational Mission**
The Educational Department's mission at the Basketball Hall of Fame is to capture the attention and imagination of youth via their love and

interest in basketball while providing learning tools and inspirational messages that teach in a fun and active learning environment.

At the Basketball Hall of Fame, we:

- Enhance students' understanding of good character by promoting proven traits that will help them make good ethical decisions and lead them on the path to success
- Inspire youth with stories of basketball celebrities who represent the traits of character that responsible and successful citizens would emulate
- Educate youth to understand the relationship between self-discipline, athletic achievement, good moral character, and how they impact academic achievement
- Apply useful life-skills education across a variety of subject. (www.hoophall.com/visitor/bhof-education-programs.html, accessed 7/7/08)

Clearly, the Hall, and its website's content, supports the connection between sports and American values and extends the metaphor of patriotism to ethics, success, responsibility, discipline and achievement in educational and social skills – each of which the Hall seeks to inspire and enhance in those who engage in the Hall experience.

The Hall is presented on the website's homepage with a view of what appears to be an induction ceremony.[1] Like many photographs on the site, this one illustrates the spherical (ball-like) structure of the Hall. The walls of this room are concave, curving in and enwrapping the guests who sit facing the speaker standing on a stage behind a podium, itself situated on a round base. The logo of the Hall sits on the far left side of the image in given position. The Hall's name is grounded in an icon of an orange and black basketball – the orange and black colors of the lettering's background paralleling the ball's colors. The word 'BASKET-BALL' is written in increasing, large, block capital font on a black background wisp, moving in an upward direction from lower left to the right side of the basketball. Just beneath are the words 'HALL OF' in an increasingly larger white font that arcs slightly from the center of the basketball icon to its right edge on an orange background. Just below these words is the word 'FAME', also in an increasingly larger white font on a black background. The word 'fame' begins just right of the center of the basketball icon and ends just to the right of the outside edge of the ball. The upward movement and progressively larger font of each of these rows of words suggests movement, as the words appear to be jutting out of the ball. The vector produced by this rightward movement draws the viewer's gaze to the rest of the image. The white font imposed on the black and orange backgrounds connote a ball in motion coming from the left and moving to the right, perhaps bouncing or being thrown from given to new position. Seemingly moving across the foreground of the photograph, the logo directs the viewer's gaze across the span of the room from audience to speaker to flags.

The Hall makes use of its rooms and displays to reinforce the image of the basketball. Roundness, however, serves more than to connote 'basketball'; roundness envelops and includes. As in the previously described picture, the Hall encircles visitors in a layout that creates a vector directed at the speaker. In turn, the website user follows this vector and also focuses on the speaker. The audience is positioned below the speaker, necessitating their looking up to view him. The website viewer must also follow this upward vector in moving his/her gaze from audience to speaker. Positioned, in this photograph, to the left and front of the speaker, this audience occupies 'real' position. They are the fans; they are the pilgrims who vastly outnumber the speaker who, in this photograph, occupies the stage that dominates the middle and right – the position, in visual semiotic analysis, of the 'ideal'.

Seated in this auditorium, the audience can also focus their gaze to the floor above on which the 'Honors Ring' gallery is located, where the Hall of Fame inductees are enshrined. It is described on its website with the following:

> (7.11) Basketball has produced a galaxy of stars, so it seems appropriate that the more than 200 elected to the Hall are displayed in a galactic ring that circles the upper floor. (www.cstv.com/ auto_pdf/p_hotos/s_chools/bhof/genrel/auto_pdf/newhall2, accessed 7/7/08)

The 'Ring' contains rectangular closeup photographs of the upper arms, shoulders and heads of Hall of Fame enshrinees. Some are dressed in their jerseys, others in suit jackets, shirts and ties. Imposed on the photograph of the Honors Ring that sits on the website is the same 'BASKETBALL HALL OF FAME' logo described above. The presence of the logo on each website photograph serves to ground each image in its habitat – each photograph is testament to the presence of its content in the Basketball Hall of Fame. The logo's presence superimposed on each photograph also brings consistency to the images – they are presented as sharing this habitat and, therefore, as collectively signifying all that is the Hall of Fame.

Once again, web viewers are encompassed by the icons of the game who themselves are enshrined in this sphere. The arc of the display suggests a room with no firm beginning or end as well as a game and its heroes who are also endless, timeless, boundless – immortal.

The photographs and biographies of these enshrinees are themselves encompassed by a white dome at the top of the museum, connoting again the celestial nature of the idealized icons eternally keeping vigil over the game and its pilgrims. The photographs surround 'Center Court' in the midst of which hangs a traditional basketball scoreboard; its screens show not game scores and times, but what are called 'Moments' – clips of memorable feats by the heroes who played the game. The floor of 'Center Court' appears made of the same kind of parquet wooden floor present in authentic basketball arenas. The expanse of empty floor space is significant; paralleling the openness of a basketball court, it invites visitors 'onto the floor' to stand beneath the scoreboard and its monitors just as basketball players do when engaged in the sport. Surrounded by the sounds and pictures of noteworthy achievements, the fan experiences

> (7.12) a sport designed for offseason physical exercise, which began with... 13 basic rules, but which has grown to become a game not for a specific culture or nation or ethnic group, but for an entire planet to share and enjoy. (http://www.hoophall.com/history/naismith-untold-story.html, accessed 7/708)

Along with the gallery in the Honors Ring, potential pilgrims can also find, through assorted links, views of displays filled with artifacts of the game's best. Uniforms, balls and other assorted game-related memorabilia accompanied by summaries and statistics can be inspected. One photograph suggests a team locker room filled with rows of grey metal lockers. These lockers, however, differ from what one might find in an actual locker room because these lockers have clear doors through which can be seen uniforms, large photographs of players and other artifacts of the game. The placement of these 'lockers' draws the viewer's gaze into the area, offering an invitation to the viewer to enter the displays – shadows that refract from the sides of the rows of lockers downward the viewer create a path into the rows between displays. The gray strips between the shadows provide similar paths to the 'larger-than-life' cutouts of renowned players, some in uniform and some dressed for other occasions, which cover the end wall of the rows. All the athletes direct their gaze toward the viewer as another vector of invitation to approach. These funnels of commitment guide the viewer into a quasi-locker room;

displays are offered in rows, metal locker doors separate individual displays. There are no tourists in this photograph; their absence conveys a hushed atmosphere worthy of a shrine; this is an environment deserving of calm, concentrated, prolonged reflection.

Another photograph found on the website also serves to invite the viewer to a display, here behind panes of glass at eye level to the tourist are collections of game jerseys and other game artifacts. Particularly significant in the visual design of this photograph is the angle at which the display case is presented, the vector drawn from the virtual tourist/ pilgrim to the display, and the absence of all but one live tourist/pilgrim in the photograph. The angle allows the right side of the display to loom large, reaching out to the viewer and taking hold of his/her attention. As the display case narrows into the background, it channels the viewer's eye to the left, inviting him/her to traverse the entire display. The pictured tourist's vector, in turn, focused upward to ideal position as well as his solitariness connotes a solemnity worthy of a shrine, a quiet area conducive to contemplation, appreciation and aspiration. In each of these photographs, the viewer/fan is brought to and into the shrines that honor the stars of the sports.

Conclusion

Addressing the role of sport in society, Young adopts a social constructivist perspective in stating,

> The solidarity function is central to a sociological understanding of sports, games, and play. We do act, feel, and think as one as we cheer, chant, despair, and rejoice together at the turns of events in the game. There can be no greater solidarity than dozens, thousands, millions thinking, doing, and feeling the same things in the same place at the same moment. These are the precious, rare moments of perfect harmony and collective exuberance in a world all too short on such moments. (Young, 1986: 8–9)

At the same time, Young acknowledges the contribution of sports to the financial economy of the community in which they are enjoyed and participated.

> In our times, sports are shaped more by the commercial needs of advanced monopoly capital. There are several points at which its needs shape the structure and development of sports. The most significant structural change in modern sports is the gradual and continuing commodification of sports. This means that the social, psychological,

physical, and cultural uses of sports are assimilated to the commercial needs of advanced monopoly capital. (Young, 1986: 12)

Sports Halls of Fame and their official websites, therefore, do more than inform prospective tourists of their mission and their artifacts. In promoting locales for tourism and for pilgrimage, these websites offer settings for honoring individuals who and activities that have contributed to the nation's pride, the culture's identity, the individual fan's identity, and the wealth and sustenance of the surrounding community. In so doing, like the tourism websites for Santiago and New Orleans, the websites for these Halls of Fame, along with being patriotic venues, have been employed to promote year-round tourism and pilgrimage as a means to restructure and maintain the economic well-being of their communities, the vitality of their sports and the interest of their fans.

Note

1. Permission to include photographs from the Basketball Hall of Fame was not granted.

Chapter 8

Balancing Promotion and Warning in the Construction of National Identity in Travel Guides: The Case of Myanmar/Burma

Introduction

One manifestation of tourist discourse not yet explored in this text exists in travel guidebooks of the sort produced by Fodor's, Michelin and, for our interests, Lonely Planet. For some researchers, travel guidebooks show evidence of doctrinal 'truths', e.g. Laderman (2002: 89) claims, 'Analyses in Western guidebooks reflect their construction by authors and editors who draw on original scholarship subscribing to disciplinary paradigms'. Additionally, as Baider *et al.* (2004: 27) note, 'The discourse of tourist guides, in its most general context, seemingly a site for the country to be visited presents itself, is in fact a place where the country of the author is also unfailingly inscribed in the glance which discursively *defines* this country'.

While the goal of this text is to examine the role of tourism websites in the construction and promotion of nations, states and attractions, a cursory exploration of travel guides serves as a relevant temporary diversion, especially in the case of the focus of this chapter.

Myanmar is a nation described by the US State Department as

(8.1) an underdeveloped, agrarian country ruled by an authoritarian military junta. The country's military government suppresses all expression of opposition to its rule. (travel.state.gov/travel/cis_pa_tw/cis/cis_1077.html, accessed 22/3/09)

Accordingly, the State Department warns potential travelers not only to

(8.2) expect to pay several times more than locals do for accommodations, domestic airfares, and entry to tourist sites... [but also] to exercise caution, register with the U.S. Embassy and check in for an update on the current security situation [and] avoid crowded public places, such as large public gatherings, demonstrations, and any area cordoned off by security forces. (travel.state.gov/travel/cis_pa_tw/pa/pa_1077.html, accessed 22/3/09)

In marked contrast, the website of the Myanmar Tourism Promotion Board explains

(8.3) Myanmar sits at the crossroads of Asia's great civilisations of India and China, and looks out onto the vast Indian Ocean next to Thailand. [It is o]ne of South East Asia's largest and most diverse countries... one of the most mysterious and undiscovered destinations in the world. A land of breathtaking beauty and charm yet only recently emerging into the modern world. (www.myanmar-tourism.com/index.htm, accessed 22/3/09)

These conflicting descriptions call for a mediator – a source that attempts to straddle the imaginary line between points of view. This is the role acknowledged by Lonely Planet on a site named 'Responsible travel' (http://www.lonelyplanet.com/about/responsible-travel, accessed 21/11/09), which is linked to the series' main webpage. As travel guides, tourism websites serve as mediators between potential tourists and destinations. They provide the linguistic and visual instruments through which content is negotiated between text and reader and ultimate tourism decisions are made. In the case of Myanmar/Burma, the Lonely Planet website for Myanmar/Burma (www.lonelyplanet.com/myanmar-burma) occupies a unique position; it also serves as a mediator for a country that has been marginalized as a result of both external and internal factors. Externally, most nations oppose the ruling junta and generally do not recognize the State Peace and Development Council's (SPDC) name change from Burma to Myanmar (see www.state.gov/r/pa/ei/bgn/35910.htm). Internally, the Union of Burma maintains a somewhat isolationist stance. To that end, the SPDC warns the Burmese to distrust outsiders. As Larkin notes,

Without any real military adversaries, the generals have had to manufacture some mythical ones. One method they have used is to evoke threats from anything or anyone considered to be non-Burmese— that is, from "the other". For example, a government billboard orders Burmese nationals to "Oppose those relying on external elements, acting as stooges, holding negative views". (Larkin, 2005: 217)

Lonely Planet is widely regarded as the travel authority, so much so that it occupies a hegemonic position in the travel guide genre (see Hallett

& Kaplan-Weinger, 2005). 'With annual sales of more than six million guidebooks–about a quarter of all the English-language guidebooks sold–it is the world's largest publisher of travel guides' (Friend, 2005: 79). Commenting on the importance of the Lonely Planet series, Pico Iyer, renowned travel writer, states, 'Lonely Planet created a floating fourth world of people who traveled full time. The guides encouraged a counter-Victorian way of life, in that they exactly reversed the old imperial assumptions. Now the other cultures are seen as the wise place, and we are taught to defer to them' (Friend, 2005: 81). Lonely Planet guides have been characterized as 'meant for the adventurous traveler who wants to live like a native [and who is] curious about the politics and culture of a destination.... The authors are opinionated and don't avoid politics' (Link, 2005: 188). Of course, in this hegemonic position, Lonely Planet is not immune to criticism for its publishing decisions. For example, 'The most serious political wrangle the company has got into is over publishing its Myanmar book despite international sanctions against that country and the stand taken by the country's Nobel Peace Prize-winning dissident, Aung San Suu Kyi, who has urged travellers to boycott the junta' (Friend, 2005: 82).

As a country undergoing civil and political change, Myanmar is in a position to construct its (late-)modern identity, one that differs radically from the identity ascribed to it by external, sanctioning forces. Not only are other nations positioning this country negatively, there are also organized movements, such as the Burma Campaign UK, otherwise positioning the country as undeserving of tourism and its benefits. Operating between these two extremes is Lonely Planet, trying not just to position itself objectively between antipodal ideologies, but also to present an ideology that promotes informed consumer decision making. Focusing on three websites that position Myanmar as a tourist destination, this chapter analyzes how Lonely Planet's web-based guide to Myanmar contrasts with both the official Myanmar tourism site and the Burma Campaign's official site (www.burmacampaign.org.uk) in presenting 'meaning in multiple articulations' (Kress & van Leeuwen, 1998: 4) – visual and linguistic – as it mediates between contrasting positions of promotion and warning.

Background

Since the 1988 uprising that was 'quelled with great severity and left many fatalities', the aforementioned ruling military junta of Myanmar has been widely denounced as an oppressive regime (Henderson, 2003: 100).

The junta has not allowed Aung San Suu Kyi, the leader of the National League for Democracy (NLD), to take office, despite the fact that her party won over 80% of the vote in the 1990 election. As a result of the government's actions, other countries have imposed sanctions against Myanmar. 'The regime, hungry for foreign cash, reacts sporadically to this international pressure, occasionally releasing political prisoners like bargaining chips or allowing Aung San Suu Kyi and her party, the NLD, more freedom to operate' (Larkin, 2005: 287). Even though the ruling junta appears not to want outside influences in Myanmar, it has come to support the development of tourism in large part due to its economic rewards (see Henderson, 2003). The 1990 Tourism Law acknowledged the importance of encouraging travel to Myanmar for national economic development; 'a second Hotel and Tourism Law in 1993 affirmed official support, setting out objectives related to the growth of the hotel and tourism sector' (Henderson, 2003: 107).

Official Myanmar Website

Not surprisingly, the official website for Myanmar positions the country as an idyllic setting for travelers. For example, the website has the following description of the country:

(8.4) Myanmar offers all the traditional delights of Asia in one fascinating country. Virgin jungles, snow-capped mountains and pristine beaches, combined with a rich and glorious heritage spanning more than two thousand years. Spectacular monuments and ancient cities attest to a vibrant culture that is still home to 135 different ethnic groups. (www.myanmar-tourism.com/, accessed 29/9/07)

Tourism is highlighted and potential fears downplayed, e.g.

(8.5) The country's tourism infrastructure boasts five star properties, intimate boutique hotels and family guest houses in all the major centers, as well as stunning mountain and beach resorts. Myanmar also boasts one of the lowest tourist crime records in the world, so visitors can rest assured their holiday will be carefree from start to finish. (www.myanmar-tourism.com/, accessed 29/9/07)

A cursory linguistic analysis of these descriptions yields positive associations through words such as 'delights', 'fascinating', 'pristine', 'rich', 'glorious', 'vibrant' and 'stunning'. Such language favorably positions Myanmar as a tourist destination offering a comfortable and attractive environment for experiencing the sights and people of Asia.

As has been argued elsewhere by the authors (see Hallett & Kaplan-Weinger, 2004a, 2004b, 2005), the linguistic text of tourism websites tells only part of the story. A rich narrative of identity is also provided by photographs and other visual texts.

Taken from the official Myanmar website, a photograph of Shwedagon Paya, a sacred Buddhist site, reinforces the above positive description, making visual text as salient as linguistic text in the positioning of Myanmar as a tourist destination[1]. In terms of visual design theory, the photograph reaches into the 'ideal' as the stupa of the temple as well as the surrounding smaller stupa direct the viewer's sight upward toward the heavens. The sky is illuminated in a red hue connoting either (if the sun is rising) a bright new day or (if the sun is setting) the forecast of a beautiful day tomorrow.

An additional photograph of the Shwedagon Pagoda, with both the daytime sky and the ground in view, positions the shrine as a bond between the earthly and heavenly. The foreground of the photograph is populated with people. Their small stature is in marked contrast to the height of the pagoda. While the stupa of the pagoda guide the viewer's gaze upward, the smallness of the people directs his/her gaze to the ground where the entrance to the shrine welcomes the human being to seek the spiritual strengths of benevolence and compassion of Buddhism.

An interesting facet of a number of the photographs on the official Myanmar website is their relatively limited focus on people. Analyses of varying photographs used in a variety of tourism materials have found either a paucity of people in the pictures (Hallett & Kaplan-Weinger, 2004a, 2004b) or their 'reduction to iconic indexes' (Baider *et al.*, 2004: 39). One explanation of this intriguing finding claims, 'The absence of people may relate to a function of objectivity... or have a metonymic function' (Baider *et al.*, 2004: 40). The pictures on the Myanmar site fall into the former category – Burma is positioned and presented as an objective locale, experienced by anyone and everyone in the same way. It is not the individual occupant or tourist that is of importance in presenting and representing Burma; it is the locale itself.

In their multimodal discourse analysis of Lithuanian tourism websites and in Chapter 4 of this text, Hallett and Kaplan-Weinger (2004a: 229) note the significance of the depiction of water in photographs on national tourism websites, stating that water connotes 'peace and tranquility' as well as vitality. This analysis makes the same claim regarding two photographs on the Myanmar site – one of Inle Lake and the other Ngapali. In responding to the 'new capitalism' of tourism, the website's integration of these photographs promotes nature and simplicity as both characteristic of the country, attractive to the tourist and, therefore, central to its economy.

The photograph of Inle Lake is of a singular male figure atop a flat boat, unfurling a large net into the lake. He is positioned just to the left of center in the middle of the vertical plane. His net unfurls to the right, centering itself in the middle of the photograph. Over the figure and the net and atop the sapphire blue sky that forms the background above the blue wave-filled waters of the lake is a horizontal row of fluffy white clouds. The clouds grow from sparse to full as they move from the viewer's left to right in the photograph. The growth of the clouds is accompanied by increased light, most likely from the sun, as the clouds turn increasingly brighter and whiter. The position of the fluffiest, whitest clouds in the right half of the photograph corresponds to the 'new' interpretation advanced in visual semiotics, suggesting Myanmar offers the tourist the kind of positive experience connoted by lightness, whiteness and softness. The presence of the lone male figure at work beneath these clouds and amidst the blue waters and blue skies also connotes a positive experience. Work is peaceful, relaxed and pleasurable in this environment.

The photograph of Ngapali, Myanmar, also promotes tranquility. Absent of human or animal figures, the photograph also offers a sapphire blue sky over a swatch of blue water positioned just beyond a short stretch of sandy beach. The sky, water and beach occupy 75% of the photograph. Taking up the entire right side as well as the top third of the photograph are palm trees, their green leafy branches hanging. Sunlight brightens the entire frame, offering a morning or daytime view. One small watercraft lies in the water, perhaps approaching the beach. Like the previous photograph, this image of nature positions Myanmar as a peaceful attraction. The viewer is led through a zone of transition – invited to the shore and the water – as the sand turns into water and the water into sky.

In contrast to these photographs, others on the Myanmar website place people in the most salient of positions. For example, two pictures each frame individuals – a lone man in one photograph and two women in the other – as they labor in the crafting of cultural artifacts. For tourists who have as one goal of travel to see native tradespeople at work, these images are quite enticing. Both photographs show the tradespeople focused on – with their respective vectors directed to – their product. As such, these photographs connote the workers' dedication to their work and the quality of their product. However, because of the vectors, the workers are disengaged from the viewer. In this physical position, the artisans represent Myanmar in an iconic, and also metonymic, manner.

These images are of particular salience in the context of the decision to participate in, rather than refrain from, travel to Myanmar. While the Myanmar Tourism Promotion Board website encourages travel to Myanmar as 'a paradise for hunting out a variety of exotic arts and crafts' (www.myanmar-tourism.com/about_myanmar.htm), Aung San Suu Kyi is quoted on the Burma Campaign website as questioning the role of tourism in bettering the lives of the citizens. She asks,

(8.6) What do these advocates of precipitate economic engagement see when they look at our country? Perhaps they merely see the picturesque scenery, the instinctive smiles with which Burmese generally greet visitors, the new hotels, the cheap labour and what appear to them as golden opportunities for making money. Perhaps they do not know of the poverty in the countryside, the hapless people whose homes have been razed to make way for big vulgar buildings, the bribery and corruption that is spreading like a cancerous growth, the lack of equity that makes the so called open market economy very open to some and hardly ajar to others, the harsh and increasingly lawless actions taken by the authorities against those who seek democracy and human rights, the forced labour projects where men, women and children toil away without financial compensation under hard taskmasters in scenes reminiscent of the infamous railway of death of the second World War. (www.burmacampaign.org.uk/aboutburma/economy.html, accessed 29/9/07)

Myanmar, as two other photographs reveal, is also constructed and promoted as a place for recreation and sports, thereby offering tourists the opportunity to see the landscape. One photograph fully frames a man on a bicycle, riding on a paved road alongside a green countryside, wheels turning such that the spokes create a blurred image. The cyclist stands above the bike seat, one leg bent, the other extended to the pedal. The bicycle's direction is to the right, into new position, suggesting, here, the kind of exploration and discovery a tourist may find attractive. The second photograph contains both a cyclist and a runner, moving along a graveled stretch of land alongside grassland. Both men wear numbered jerseys (of the sort participants in a race wear) atop t-shirts. These men, the runner in full stride, as suggested by the front of the shoe on his forward foot lifted slightly off the ground and the back leg bent backward with its foot in the air, and the cyclist pedaling, as suggested by his leaning posture over the handlebars and his legs in bent position on the pedals, also participate in leisure, perhaps competitive, activity. Their participation signifies Myanmar's construction and its website's promotion as a place not just for experiencing long existent spiritual traditions in populated settings, but also more modern physical activities to be participated in open, undeveloped areas. The tranquility suggested by these settings is somewhat incongruous in the context of the following warning issued by the US State Department regarding travel to Myanmar:

> (8.7) some tourists traveling to places where permission is not expressly required have reported delays due to questioning by local security personnel... Individuals planning to travel in Burma should check with Burmese tourism authorities to see whether travel to specific destinations is permitted. Even if the Burmese authorities allow travel to specific destinations in Burma, it may not be safe to travel in those areas. (travel.state.gov/travel/cis_pa_tw/cis/cis_1077.html)

Myanmar/Burma, in its contrasting positioning by self and by Other, offers a unique paradigm for the analysis of tourism and the websites that promote or discourage it. Atop the homepage of the Burma Campaign UK website is an icon printed on a horizontal field of burgundy or saffron spanning the entire width of the page (Photo 8.1). The words 'Burma Campaign UK' are written in white on the saffron background with the unevenly shaded frame remaining black. To the left of the icon are the words 'for Human Rights, Democracy and Development in Burma', also printed in white on the saffron background. Only in the context of the political strife existing in this region is this site and its content understandable. A link calling for a global arms embargo against Burma labels 'The dictatorship in Burma [as] one of the most brutal in the world' (http://www.burmacampaign.org.uk/). Burma Campaign UK self-identifies as 'one of the leading Burma campaign organisations in the world' (http://www.burmacampaign.org.uk/).

Photo 8.1 Burma Campaign webpage banner (www.burmacampaign.org.uk/, accessed 28/2/09)

Significantly, visitors to the site are met with a particular political stance, if only indirectly, before they continue reading. First, by framing its content in saffron, the Campaign integrates the color of the robes worn by Buddhist monks who oppose the ruling junta. Additionally, by using the name 'Burma', the campaign refuses to recognize the ruling junta's attempt to rename and thus, reinvent the country as Myanmar. This campaign, which for the purposes of our analysis represents attempts to effect social action through the promotion of tourism, appears to recognize the importance of tourism in the new capitalism:

(8.8) Why the ruling army junta, the State Peace and Development Council (known from 1988–1997 as the State Law and Order Restoration Council, or SLORC), wants more tourists to come to Burma is no secret. The generals themselves declare that gaining hard currency is their prime motivation. They also hope that a large influx of international tourists will raise global respectability and credibility for a military dictatorship with one of the world's worst human rights records. (www.burmacampaign.org.uk/index.php/ burma/about-burma/about-burma/tourism, accessed 7/11/09)

Also on the Burma Campaign UK website is a human rights link. Its contents begin as follows:

(8.9) Since an army coup overthrew Burma's last democratically-elected government in 1962, military-run or dominated regimes in Burma have been among the world's worst violators of human rights. An already serious level of abuses climbed higher after the State Law and Order Restoration Council (SLORC) (renamed the State Peace and Development Council in November 1997) seized power in September 1988. The junta removed all pretence of civilian admin-istration and marked its arrival by massacring thousands of unarmed pro-democracy demonstrators in Rangoon and other Burmese cities and towns. Today, says Amnesty International, "torture has become an institution" in Burma. Reports by the United Nations, Amnesty International, Human Rights Watch, and other groups have repeatedly detailed a gruesome litany of abuses, including murder, torture, rape, detention without trial, massive forced relocations, and forced labor.

This linguistic text marks the intense command of the ruling government, focusing on actions it has taken leading to the torture and death of Burmese. The text positions the government as constraining and excessively brutal. The following text, in turn, positions the political protestors and prisoners as suffering greatly from these actions. They were punished 'just for peacefully calling for democracy and freedom'. They endure undeservingly severe treatment.

> (8.10) There are over 2,200 political prisoners in Burma. They have been imprisoned just for peacefully calling for democracy and freedom in Burma. Once in prison, democracy activists face horrific torture, including electric shocks, rape, iron rods rubbed on their shins until the flesh rubs off, severe beatings and solitary confinement. Many prisoners are kept in their cells 24 hours a day, given inadequate food and are in poor health. However, the regime appears to be systematically denying medical treatment to political prisoners. (http://www.burmacampaign.org.uk/index.php/campaigns/free-political-prisoners/14/53)

Also notable in the Burma Campaign is their attempt to encourage participation in the protest by those who explore their website. Appealing to the same electronic media they employ to make their position known (just as that employed by the Myanmar government), the Campaign encourages outside participation in the protests and larger social action and support through e-mailing, electronic petition signing and Facebook posting.

Aung San Suu Kyi, Nobel Peace Prize winner, leader of Burma's democracy movement, and political prisoner for more than 14 years urges a tourism boycott. Her 1995 statement reprinted on the website reads 'We think it is too early for either tourists or investment or aid to come pouring into Burma ...We would like to see that these things are conditional on genuine progress towards democratization'. In 2002, Aung San Suu Kyi reiterated her call for a tourism boycott. In an interview with the BBC, she said: 'Our policy with regard to tourism has not changed, which is to say that we have not yet come to the point where we encourage people to come to Burma as tourists' (http://www.burmacampaign.org.uk/index.php/burma/about-burma/about-burma/tourism).

In addition to forging its own campaign to deter tourism to Burma, the Burma Campaign UK website encourages potential tourists to protest the Lonely Planet tour guides whose guide to Burma, they claim, contributes to the torment and anguish of the Burmese population.

> (8.12) Lonely Planet Targeted over New Burma Guide 05 Nov 2002 Remembrance vigil for victims of tourism in Burma to be held outside Lonely Planet HQ On Friday 8th November, 8.30–10am Burma Campaign UK (BCUK) will hold a remembrance vigil for

those who have suffered as a direct result of tourism to Burma. The vigil will coincide with the publication of a new edition of Lonely Planet's guide to Burma. BCUK calls for a tourist boycott of Burma, and for the tourism industry to stop promoting the country as a holiday destination.

"Tourism provides a vital source of income for the military dictatorship in Burma", says Yvette Mahon, Director of BCUK. "Lonely Planet's guide encourages people to visit Burma, going against the wishes of the democratic movement in Burma." (/www.burmacampaign.org.uk/ index.php/news-and-reports/news-stories/ Lonely-Planet-Targeted-over-New-Burma-Guide, accessed 7/11/09)

Another use of linguistic text, as well as visual text, to thwart tourism is found in a picture on the campaign's website. Visual design theory (Kress & van Leeuwen, 1998) explains that the layout of components within a visual text conveys meaning. The theory as it applies to this image offers us, first, the contrast between given and new. If we divide Photo 8.2 vertically in half, we find BUR written in a standard uppercase block font. The font is imposed over the blue background of the sky and ocean. The viewer's eye is drawn first to the BUR because of its left-most position and its brightness. This part of the work is salient, but only until one's eyes continue along the left-to-right plane. Seemingly written in

Photo 8.2 Burma Campaign 'advertisement' (www.burmacampaign.org.uk/ tourism.php, accessed 29/9/07)

blood, the 'MA' connotes a number of meanings: injury, death, mutilation, torture, clawing. One might wonder whether the hand is writing in one's own blood or in the blood of another. The 'given' message is that Burma is a bright, tropical place; the 'new' message is that Burma – like the word itself – has been injured. The presence and position of the hand indicates that the blood is fresh, as is the injury.

Dividing the photograph in half horizontally, we see a contrast in lighting. The bottom half of the image suggests sunshine, warmth and relaxation. The top half is both dark in lighting and in theme. We are not unfamiliar with speaking of travel with the terms 'cost of a holiday'. When juxtaposed with the word 'life', 'cost' connotes, as it does in financial contexts, worth and value. The statement 'The cost of a holiday can be someone's life' serves as a warning and plea against travel to Burma. The claim is that in traveling to Burma, the tourist supports the regime that suppresses the masses.

The Burma campaign does not rely solely on linguistic texts to argue against travel to Burma. Visual images are also employed to discourage tourism. Photo 8.3, also from the Burma Campaign website, adopts and adapts a familiar icon of travel – the luggage tag.

Rather than providing open space for one's name and address, the tag assumes the voice of the tourist, using uppercase font to stress the message and a color change to black to further stress the inaction. Saffron again is a dominant color, filling in both the background and the majority of the lettering. This color choice might pronounce a metaphor for Buddhism and its teachings as well as for blood and, therefore, peril; it may also, in an American cultural context connote the color of the 'stop'

Photo 8.3 Burma Campaign logo (www.burmacampaign.org.uk/imnotgoing pledges.htm, accessed 20/9/07)

traffic sign. The inaction called for in this text actually translates into action – social action – with the force of the imperative prompted at the bottom of the tag.

Lonely Planet

The Lonely Planet website for Myanmar/Burma (this title, itself, a bow to mediation) recognizes the debate by juxtaposing the two conflicting stances.

> (8.14) Isolated and ostracised by the international community, the country is in the grip of tyrants. Most travellers avoid a visit, backing the boycott, but the long-suffering people are everything the regime is not. Gentle, humorous, engaging, considerate and inquisitive, they want to play a part in the world, and deserve a brighter future. ... Travelling to Myanmar presents an ethical decision – should you go?

Inviting potential travelers to Burma to investigate the nation and the dilemma more fully, the website contains a link to the Lonely Planet tour book chapter titled 'Should You Go?' Here, the site lists eight reasons not to go followed by seven reasons to go (http://www.lonelyplanet.com/ shop_pickandmix/free_chapters/myanmar-10-should-you-go.pdf).

Lonely Planet's ultimate stance is stated thus: 'Lonely Planet believes all prospective visitors must ask, and answer, this question for themselves'. It offers, however, for those who choose to travel to Burma, advice on how 'to keep the bulk of your money in private hands' (http:// www.lonelyplanet.com/shop_pickandmix/free_ chapters/myanmar-10-should-you-go.pdf).

Navigating through the Myanmar 'Overview' and 'Our Top Picks for Myanmar and Burma' site links, the viewer comes upon links to pages devoted to major areas, cities and attractions. Some descriptions also address the political conflict. For example, lead text on the Yangon/ Rangoon site reads:

> Vibrant and dynamic, sweaty and steamy, reaching for the future but trapped in the past, Yangon is a fascinating introduction to Myanmar. It's diverse too – home to Burmese, Shan, Mon, Chinese, Indians and Western expats. Aung San Suu Kyi remains under house arrest here in her home on University Ave. General Than Shwe is rumoured to return on weekends, perhaps unable to survive the boredom of sterile Naypyidaw, the new "capital". (http://www.lonelyplanet.com/ myanmar-burma/yangon-rangoon, accessed 21/11/09)

Others, like the following text on the Mandalay site, ignore the conflict.

Poetic though the name may be, Mandalay is a thoroughly modern city, the second largest in the country. The dusty streets sprawl east of the Ayeyarwady and south of Mandalay Hill, a stupa-studded hill looming over the flat cityscape. It's impossible not to be impressed by the golden Buddha of Mahamuni Paya, but the real attractions lie beyond town in the nearby ancient cities. (http://www.lonelyplanet. com/myanmar-burma/Mandalay)

Therefore, while we recognize the attempt by Lonely Planet to mediate between the stances as it frames objective information about the city in a statement of advice to the traveler, the site positions itself more as an objective source of travel and tourist information rather than as a promoter of caution, or even refutation, of tourist action.

Conclusion

As Henderson (2003) notes, tourism can serve as both a tool and a weapon. In the case of Myanmar, tourism can be a tool for infusing new capital into an economically disadvantaged area and a weapon for combating a hostile regime. This analysis argues that these competing metaphors apply not only to tourism, but also to tourism discourse. The official Myanmar website seeks to use discourse as a tool to solicit much-needed funds through tourism. By contrast, the Burma Campaign uses tourism discourse as a weapon to attack the ruling junta. In its position between, Lonely Planet clearly sees the flexibility of tourism discourse in mediating between these perspectives, choosing to offer its readers both sides of the issue. The extent to which they present a balanced or unbiased view, however, is a matter of interpretation.

Note

1. Permission was not granted to use photographs from the official Myanmar website.

Chapter 9
Constructing Self versus Other in Parodic Travel Guides

As we have established in the previous chapters, official tourism websites have become an established genre of travel writing. As with all other established genres, this particular style of writing is subject to parody (see Nilsen & Nilsen, 2000), even though humor is not typical on official tourism websites. In this chapter, we argue that the website for the fictitious nations of Molvania, Phaic Tan and San Sombrèro (www.molvania.com) exploits the conventions of this particular travel genre by using different yet compatible, opposite yet overlapping scripts (see Raskin, 1985). Intertextuality and hegemony, key to understanding the humor passages in this parody, are the foci of our analysis. Recognition of our stereotypes makes us aware of the hegemonic weight of our own worldviews and cultural values. Our analysis shows how parodic travel guides (re)present self and Other by reinforcing stereotypes of what it means to be hegemonic and central (as opposed to exotic and peripheral), even when content is fictitious.

Parody 'has been defined as a subspecies of satire, the genre of making-fun-of' (Chatman, 2001: 28). As a technique, parody can either denigrate or praise. A recent example of textual parody is the *Jetlag Travel Guide* series, which illustrates how humor can evolve out of the adoption of style but not subject matter (see Chatman, 2001), in this case, by adopting the travel genre style for fictitious locales. For Buzard (1993: 7), parody in this genre may be the result of 'the product of anti-tourist rhetoric': '"the tourist" and his or her domain represent the sinister or parodic double to many modern wishes about culture and acculturation'. In a similar vein, Dann (1996: 181) notes, 'From abhorrence of cultural practices of the Other, it is but a short step to the explicit denigration of all locals, a familiar enough theme in travel writing, but somehow made more acceptable by the injection of patronizing humour'.

Returning to Laderman's (2002) notion of doctrinal 'truths', we need to ask what 'truths' are to be found in a parody of an official tourism website. The analysis of the Jetlag Travel Guide website for Molvania, Phaic Tan and San Sombrèro adopts Hutcheon's (1989: 94, original emphasis) notion that 'parody works to foreground the *politics* of the accepted view of representation'. Hutcheon (1989: 94) continues, 'postmodernist parody is a value-problematizing, de-naturalizing form of acknowledging the history (and through irony, the politics) of representations'.

When providing a narrative of a nation, it becomes important to distinguish between the self and the Other. As Bhabha (1990: 4) explains, 'the "other" is never outside or beyond us: it emerges forcefully, within cultural discourse, when we *think* we speak most intimately and indigenously "between ourselves"'. If it is true that a community constructs identity and power from what it agrees upon as being normal, standard, natural or unmarked, thus providing for itself the co-construction and co-recognition of hegemonic positioning from their practice of 'normalcy', then we should be able to identify the parodic components of a text as those that question the other's normalcy.

Stereotyping an Eastern European Identity: Molvania

An initial source of humor comes from parodying the homepage of an official tourism website and the cover of a travel guide. The homepage of www.molvania.com contains pictures of the print versions of three parodic travel guides published by Jetlag Travel: *Molvania: A Land Untouched by Modern Dentistry* (Cilauro *et al.*, 2003), *Phaic Tan: Sunstroke on a Shoestring* (Cilauro *et al.*, 2004) and *San Sombrèro: A Land of Carnivals, Cocktails and Coups* (Cilauro *et al.*, 2006). Clicking on copies of the books takes the visitor to the website and the official page for that 'country'. As the main page for Molvania, 'one of Eastern Europe's most overlooked destinations' (according to the inside cover of the print version), an instrumental version of the Molvanian national anthem begins to play. Immediately, the viewer realizes that the book is a parody as there are quotes from *Time Out*, the *Spectator* and *The Daily Telegraph*, stating how funny the book is. Even the cover of the book contains the following quote from Bill Bryson: 'Brilliantly original and very, very funny'. Along the left-hand side of the page are the following links: 'Background', 'Culture & Entertainment', 'Useful Facts', 'FAQ', 'Photo Gallery', Buy the Book', 'Upcoming Titles', 'Reviews', 'Publicity Enquiries', 'Press Releases', 'Links' and a map of Molvania. The last of these links, i.e. the map, depicts four regions of the country with six statements, e.g. 'Molvania's capital Lutenblag – where old world charm meets concrete' and 'The colourful Spring Festival of the Eastern Steppes where each year adolescent boys serenade a mule' (http://www.molvania.com.au/molvania/map.html, accessed 20/10/08).

The cover of the parody focuses on an aged man with bushy eyebrows and a wide, open smile marked by the absence of some teeth and bloody gums, offering the reader/viewer a shot of 'zeerstum', or 'garlic brandy', which, according to the description on the inside flap, is 'traditionally served for breakfast in many parts of the country'. Through the man's salience in the picture, the reader is led to personify this fictitious Eastern European country. The use of such an image in travel guides for Eastern European countries, however, is very marked. In our earlier analysis of Lithuanian tourism websites, we found an absence of individual people (Hallett & Kaplan-Weinger, 2004a). When people are found in travel guides, as Yarymowich (2004) states, they have 'youthful, smiling faces, assuming an advertising and persuasive function as symbols of pleasure' (cited in Baider *et al.*, 2004: 40). While the Molvanian man here is smiling, he is hardly a youthful advertisement for his homeland. Are we to assume, then, that he, his drink and his surroundings (mis)represent a stereotype of an Eastern European identity?

As we have discussed elsewhere, it is common for official tourism websites to provide information about the local language(s). Titular language is closely associated with identity (see Ciscel *et al.*, 2002; Hallett & Kaplan-Weinger, 2004a). This commonly known feature thus becomes the subject of parody on the Molvanian website:

(9.1) Molvanian is a difficult language to speak, let alone master. There are **four genders**: male, female, neutral, and the collective noun for cheeses, which occupies a nominative sub-section of its very own. The language also contains numerous **irregular verbs**, archaic phrases, words of multiple meaning, and several phonetic sounds linguists suspect could represent either a rare dialect or merely peasants clearing their throat. (www.molvania.com.au/molvania/useful.html, original emphasis, accessed 20/10/08)

In this example, we see a focus on the archaism of the languages, a feature of singularization that, according to the model put forth by Wodak *et al.*, adds to the construction of a national identity by distinguishing one nation and its language as unique. At the same time, we see the exotic Other portrayed in the description of the syntax of Molvanian:

(9.2) Remember, too, that the syntactical structure of written Molvanian can be rather complex, with writers routinely using the **triple negative.** Hence,
'Can I drink the water?'

becomes *'Erkjo ne szlepp statsik ne var ne vladrobzko ne'*
(literally, 'is it not that the water is not not undrinkable?')
(http://www.molvania.com.au/molvania/useful.html, original emphasis, accessed 20/10/2008)

Following this grammatical explanation are lists of 'Common Expressions', such as the Molvanian for 'Where is the toilet paper?' and 'What
happened to your teeth?', as well as 'Less Common Expressions', such as
the Molvanian translations for 'More food, inn-keeper' and 'What
beautiful children!' Again, through these examples, Molvania and, by
extension, Eastern European countries are parodied as exotic Others,
places that are inhospitable, unattractive and possibly dangerous to a
tourist's health.

Parodying Southeast Asian Tourism: Phaic Tan

The humor on the webpages for the fictitious Southeast Asian nation
of Phaic Tan also draws on similar material. The main webpage again
offers a picture of the cover of the print version of the travel parody
along with the statement 'The hilarious follow-up to the international
bestseller MOLVANIA' (http://www.jetlagtravel.com/phaic_tan/, accessed 20/10/08). As is the case with the cover of the Molvanian text,
the Phaic Tan text features a man with less-than-perfect dentistry
(Photo 9.1).

On the left-hand side of the webpage are the following links:
'Background', 'The Royal Family', 'Getting Round', 'Cuisine', 'Flora &
Fauna', 'Phaic Tan after Dark', 'Sport', 'Health & Safety', 'Publicity
Enquiries', 'Buy the Book' and a map of Phaic Tan. The map includes
four regions, each of which involves a linguistic play on words:
Sukkondat (Suck on that?), which is described as the province 'where
happy farmers harvest hay in order to camouflage their primary crop,
opium'; Pha Phlung (Far Flung?), the province 'renowned for its
rainforests and spectacular mud-slides'; Bhung Lung (Bung Lung?),
'where all car horns have cruise control, set to go off every 10 seconds';
and Thong On, 'a beach-lovers' paradise, where sea meets souvenir
shop' (http://www.jetlagtravel.com/phaic_tan/map.htm, accessed
20/10/08). The capital is the onomatopoeic 'Bumpattabumpah'.

In order to appreciate the humor found in the section on the royal
family, the website visitor must appreciate the intertextuality found
there. Under a portrait of His Majesty Sukhimbol Tralanhng III and his
wife, Her Royal Highness Queen Suahm Luprang, is a description of the
royal couple's children, among them Princess Buk Phang and Prince

Photo 9.1 Phaic Tan guidebook cover (www.jetlagtravel.com/phaic_tan/, accessed 20/10/08)

Luat. The text about the princess reads, 'Known as "the People's Princess", she is rarely seen in public' (http://www.jetlagtravel.com/phaic_tan/royal.htm, accessed 20/10/08). The moniker 'People's Princess' brings to mind the description of the late Diana, Princess of Wales. Prince Luat is described in the following manner:

(9.3) The youngest member of the Royal Family is **Prince Luat** ("Luat the Brooding") who, unfortunately, made headlines a few years ago when he walked into the palace during a state function armed with a semi automatic pistol and opened fire. Mercifully, due to Luat's extreme short-sightedness he failed to hit a single family member; however, the Royal Dog sustained serious leg wounds and had to be eaten. Shortly after, Prince Luat was committed to Phaic Tan's newest psychiatric hospital, named in his honour. (www.jetlagtravel.com/ phaic_tan/royal.htm, accessed 20/10/08)

The story of the assassination attempt reminds informed readers of Nepalese Crown Prince Diprenda's attack on his family in the Narayanhity Royal Palace on 1 June 2001; ten people were killed and five were wounded. The passage also plays on (an)other stereotype: the alleged consumption of dog in Asian cultures.

Though not found on the website for Phaic Tan, the written and visual texts in the print version of the parodic travel guide focuses on the hegemonic notion of normal (i.e. non-exotic) food. In the case of Southeast Asian travel, there is a commonly held stereotype of eating dog. The Phaic Tan travel guide plays on this stereotype with the following description and picture:

> (9.4) You won't travel far in Phaic Tan without coming across a restaurant or street stall selling dog. While many foreigners are appalled by this practice, the Phaic Tanese think nothing of it and serve their four-legged friends up in a **dazzling range** of culinary creations. If you do order dog (*lah-see*) you're likely to be presented with its liver, barbecued hind legs, spicy shoulder sausage or minced intestines. Diners unable to finish their meal may take the left–overs home in a **doggy bag**, often made out of the animal's stomach. (Cilauro *et al.*, 2004b: 49, original emphasis)

In terms of linguistic word play, humor in this passage is found in the Phaic Tanese gloss for 'dog', *lah-see*, as well as in the use of the term 'doggy bag'. In the former, the fake Phaic Tanese word provides an intertextual reference to a popular American television program featuring a dog named 'Lassie'. Even the pronunciation of the dog's name has been made more exotic; in most dialects of English, the first vowel of 'lassie' is the low front lax unrounded vowel /æ/. Regarding the use of the term 'doggy bag', we see an ambiguity – 'doggy bag', traditionally, is a bag full of food for one's dog; in this context, it is instead a bag full of and made out of dog (Photo 9.2).

> (9.5) DOG GONE IT!
> Many western visitors to Phaic Tan are terrified of the possibility that they may – even accidentally – end up eating dog. A good test when served any roast meat is to look closely at the animal's head. While pigs and goats will traditionally have an apple stuffed in their mouth, dogs tend to be cooked holding a tennis ball. (Cilauro *et al.*, 2004b: 49)

Photo 9.2 Phaic Tanese cuisine (http://www.phaic-tan.de/photos/p49.jpg, accessed 11/7/09)

'Exotic food' is, of course, a major draw for many tourists and is commonly part of the contents of traditional travel guides. For example, the Lonely Planet guide for Myanmar in its section on 'Facts for the Visitor – Health' writes these 'Basic Rules' for food: 'There is an old colonial adage which says: "If you can cook it, boil it or peel it you can eat it—otherwise forget it"' (Martin *et al.*, 2002: 97). If we compare the parodic version, we see the same adage with only slight modification: 'With fruit and vegetables, follow the **old adage:** Boil it, cook it, peel it and then throw it away' (Cilauro *et al.*, 2004b: 50, original emphasis). This is another example of borrowing, recontextualizing and modifying a hegemonic source to create humor.

Satirizing Central America: San Sombrèro

As seen in the Molvanian and Phaic Tanese websites, the website for the fictitious country of San Sombrèro also plays on stereotypes of the Other or the exotic. On the first page of the website, we find a picture of the book, which – like the other parodies – depicts a man who is supposed to represent this fictitious nation (Photo 9.3).

Similar to the Phaic Tan website, the links on the left side of the page are the following: 'Home', 'Portrait of San Sombrèro', 'Special Events & Festivals', 'The People', 'Food and Drink', 'Political Structure', 'Sport',

Photo 9.3 San Sombrèro guidebook cover (www.molvania.com/sansombrero/, accessed 20/12/07)

'Music', 'Hot Guide', 'Podcasts & Downloads', 'The Jetlag Story', 'Public Enquiries', 'Buy the Book' and an interactive map. When the page comes up, a song, the 'bababumba', begins to play. The information on this webpage defines the bababumba as 'steamy' and 'one of the few dances in the world to routinely involve an exchange of body fluids' (www.molvania.com/sansombrero/, accessed 25/03/09). The source of humor in the place names and descriptions on the map is twofold: linguistic word play and cultural stereotyping. The regions include Lambara (Lambada?), where 'The beach resort town of Aguazura is home of the first ever **Madame Tussaud's Brazilian Wax Museum**'; San Abandonio (St Abandon?), where 'Visitors flock to Nicotiño's (Nicotine?)

famous **Tomb of the Unpaid Soldier**'; Maracca (Maraca?), where 'Innovative farmers… have recently produced the world's first crop of **decaffeinated cocaine**'; Guacomala (Guacamole?), in which 'Cohlera's magnificent **Cathedral of San Pedro** is noted for its massive organ, as was he'; and Polluçión (Pollution?), which contains the capital, Cucaracha (Spanish for 'cockroach') City. In the use of faux and real Spanish terms as well as diacritics not found in English (e.g. ñ, ç and ó), the creators of the website have chosen to emphasize the exotic.

The political structure of Central American countries is also parodied throughout this website. Describing the country as a 'totalinocracy', the website explains that the nation of San Sombrèro is 'ruled over by an elected President answerable to the National Assembly of Right Wing Death Squads' (www.molvania.com/sansombrero/political.html, accessed 20/12/07). Following a further description of the government, the website offers a flowchart (see Photo 9.4).

Similar to the other two parodic guides, this guide to San Sombrèro also portrays the local/regional food as exotic. For example, the following description from the Food and Drink link states,

> (9.6) Whilst San Sombrèro may not be the **food-lovers** [sic] ultimate destination, it is **possible** to eat well – and cheaply – throughout the country. Traditional San Sombrèran food *(criollo)* takes a range of **culinary influences** – Spanish, African, indigenous – and basically adds coconut. Fish (pescado) and **chicken** (pollo) are the most common **meats**, closely followed by rabbit *(rodekil)*. (www.molvania.com/sansombrero/food.html, accessed 20/12/07)

While rabbit may not be considered an exotic meat in the Anglophone world, its exoticness is played up in the addition of the faux Spanish term for it, 'rodekil', which is clearly an imitation of the English term 'roadkill'. Adding to the exoticism of this section, the website continues to explain the difficulties vegetarian travelers to the country might have:

> (9.7) It's not easy eating meat-free in San Sombrèro as even simple vegetable dishes will often have meat added to "improve" them. Rice and beans are routinely fried in animal fat or boiled in stock that has had an animal bone or organ added for extra flavour. Even so-called "vegetarian" restaurants will generally include chicken on the menu. If stuck, your best bet is to simply drink bottled water (although avoid *Agua Toro* as it may contain small amounts of beef stock). http:// www.molvania.com/sansombrero/food.html, accessed 25/3/09)

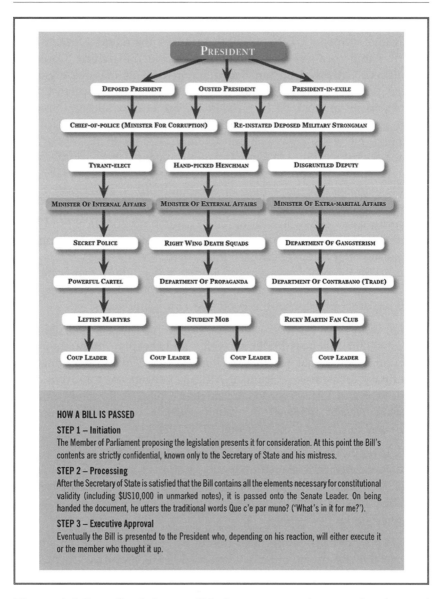

Photo 9.4 San Sombrèro political structure (www.molvania.com/ sansombrero/political.html, accessed 20/12/07)

Photo 9.5 Rotulos de huevos, San Sombrèro (www.molvania.com/ sansombrero/food.html, accessed 20/12/07)

English speakers who are familiar with Spanish will probably get the intertextual humor of the phrase 'Agua Toro'; 'agua' is the Spanish for 'water' and 'toro' is the Spanish for 'bull'. In their parody, the website creators have even linguistically (re)created a Spanish term.

Pictures (and their accompanying texts) further enforce the parodic nature of this exotic cuisine. For example, the text, "Rotulos de huevos is a typical sweet similar to licorice except it is made out of rubber" is accompanied by Photo 9.5.

Likewise, Photo 9.6 accompanies the text, "Donkey and mule meat is used extensively – especially as an appetizer. This is known locally as "Hee Haw D'oeuvre"'.

Lastly, the stereotype of travelers' succumbing to stomach problems after eating Central American cuisine is also highlighted in this section, as seen in the explanation of 'potaje': 'a thick oily soup made from black beans, with fried garlic, onion, pepper and chilli. It is generally served before a main course or a colonoscopy' and warning:

Photo 9.6 Hee Haw D'oeuvre, San Sombrèro (www.molvania.com/sansombrero/food.html, accessed 20/12/07)

(9.8) While the cost of eating out in San Sombrèro is generally quite low, so too are the hygiene standards, and diners struck by the sudden onset of gastro-intestinal illness during the middle of a meal may find themselves subject to a 10% "corkage charge". (www.molvania.com/sansombrero/food.html, accessed 20/12/07)

Also satirized in this website is the character of the natives of San Sombrèro. The Western stereotypes of the passionate, beautiful people of Central America are reinforced:

(9.9) But more than anything else, it is the people of San Sombrèro who many regard as the "main" attraction, and first-time visitors are

Photo 9.7 San Sombrèro uniforms (www.molvania.com/sansombrero/portrait.html, accessed 20/12/07)

invariable struck by the natural **beauty** of its citizens. This country where ugliness (or *"aranche"*) is officially classified as a **disability** and even prisoners have **solarium rights**. The San Sombreran women, in particular, proudly flaunt their looks and sexuality, with baby girls often learning to **shimmy** before they can walk. And, despite moves to ban the practice, female **soldiers** serving in San Sombreran regiments frequently disobey orders by re-designing their combat uniforms to create a bare midriff. (www.molvania.com/sansombrero/portrait.html, accessed 20/12/07)

Below the text, Photo 9.7, with the caption 'Female members of San Sombrèro's armed forces model their latest camouflage uniforms', appears.

Conclusion

Parody, as demonstrated in this analysis, is a unique type of humor. In parodying one text, the other pays homage to and authorizes its legitimacy. Parodic travel guides, such as the one we have examined, demonstrate the established existence of the travel guide genre while reinforcing the hegemonic role of such guides in helping one determine where to travel. Concomitantly, parodic travel guides strengthen our perceptions of self versus other in confirming our normalcy compared to others' exoticness.

Chapter 10

Conclusion: On Tourism, Identity and the World Wide Web

> Representations are integral to tourism and the tourist industry. Symbols, images, signs, phrases and narratives provide the ideas that fuel the commodification and consumption of tourist sites. Representations are disseminated by souvenirs, travel guides, postcards, travel accounts, photography, guidebooks, travel programmes and in a host of popular cultural forms including televised and cinematic drama, news bulletins and lifestyle magazines. (Edensor, 2002: 13)

It is clear that tourism websites and the representations they incorporate provide this fuel as well. Hummon (1988: 180) explains 'Because tourism involves consumption outside of the normal round of life, advertising is particularly important for providing symbolic representations for status display that would otherwise be socially invisible in everyday lives'. It is also clear, as the analyses in this text have illustrated, that representations are also integral to identity construction. Beyond fueling tourism as commodity and tourism for consumption, the representations that inhabit tourism websites fuel those who consume these commodities as well as the very locales that are consumed. Through the interactive process of creating and consuming tourism websites, these representations are given meaning by the potential tourists who explore them; at the same time, these potential tourists are engaged through this interaction in the construction of self as tourist and of locale as tourism site.

How do tourism websites with their various linguistic and visual texts and design components function to construct identities for their users and for the promoted locales? How do potential tourists maintain that identity as well as construct the identity of virtual tourists – perhaps ultimately actual tourists – constructed by these sites? And how do these personal identities shift as the websites shift? These questions of correlation have engaged us from our pre-writing, and our actualized tourist days, through our continued touring – both virtually and actualized – as we pursued the role of tourism researchers in writing this text.

What tourism websites do for a nation, state or other destination in constructing it as a tourist locale, endowing it with salience through its attractions and attractiveness, the virtual representations of the locale do for the prospective tourist. Operating in what we earlier cited as a binary mode of real virtuality (Castells, 2000), the creators and purveyors of these websites endow locales with the potential for distinction, recognition, rebirth and reconstruction. At the same time, as those purveyors come to play a seminal role in the maintenance and reformation of these locales, they are bestowed with an identity of economic, social and/or political redeemer. Identity has been defined both within this text and the larger body of social constructionist literature as mutually defined and mediated through multiple modes of interaction and as fluid in creation and re-creation. Relevant to critical discourse analysis, identity is concomitant with social action and independence in reference to a presentation of self that is at once favorable to and autonomous from others. (In politeness theory, this is a self or face that is presented and preserved through both positive and negative acts (Brown & Levinson, 1987).) These theoretical constructs mesh well with an exploration of electronic media and Web texts, for as Fürsich and Robins (2004: 140–141) explain, 'The non-linear and ephemeral aspects of Web content resonate with cultural-critical scholars' poststructuralist concept of "text" as an unsettled, open, and shifting process of meaning making never fully fixed between encoding and decoding (Barthes, 1975; Hall, 1980)'.

In their discussion of researching the Web, Schneider and Foot (2004: 114–115) echo Fürsich and Robins in characterizing the Web as 'a unique mixture of the ephemeral and the permanent'. Schneider and Foot (2004: 115) explain that the Web exhibits ephemerality in 'its transience, as it can be expected to last for only a relatively brief time'. For the Web user, whose identity is co-constructed with the website's identity, this growth and change results in an ever-shifting identity in concord with the site's ever-changing content and form. For the website itself, as well, ephemerality breeds alteration. Diamandaki (2003) explains

> Another particularity of the depiction of identity online is that it is too malleable to be durable and consistent. Constructed by the input and discourses of its member-users, any digital nation is subject to the ephemerality that stems from the a-temporal nature of cyber-discourse. How durable and coherent can the digital image of a nation be in the ever-changing nature of cyberspace? The digital

image of a national, ethnic or for that matter any identity, is in a way doomed to be a "metamorphosising image [...] since every single posting changes the image to some degree and this change is a continuing process since the postings never stop" (Mitra, 1997, p. 75). It may feel palpable, but is always fleeting and evanescent, permanently open to reproduction and change in the light of the mobile nature of cyber-discourse.

Through linguistic and visual semiotic codes, these tourism sites foster social action that contributes to the (re)construction of nations and other communities by variably fostering re-imagination, rebirth, renaissance, promotion and caution, and patriotism. Social action is a process that itself leads to a product most often viewed, within the framework of critical discourse analysis, as a positive social contribution. Social action, however, is also a product. As we have examined the role, as well as the structures, of tourism websites, we have demonstrated that it is through the cooperative, negotiative, mediated interaction of websites and tourists that identities for destinations and their visitors are constructed. Without the mutual design of these identities, there would be no foundation from which could spring the accomplishment of social action contributing to the rebirth of New Orleans and other locales in Louisiana and of Gary, Indiana; the education of outsiders to the nation of and the political unrest in Myanmar (Burma); the promotion of pilgrimage sites such as Santiago de Compostela; the re-construction of national identity in the Baltic nations; the igniting of patriotism and nationalism through sports and their athletes; and the comprehension of parodic discourse in the representation of truly 'imagined' communities.

The journey that is tourism has much in common with the metaphorical journey that is life. Most notably, both journeys result in the transformation of one's identity. As we have explored identity in this text, we have followed the foundation set by social constructionists and social interactionists who theorize identity as built upon 'both the structures of everyday lives and the sociocultural and sociopolitical realities in which those lives are lived' (Howard, 2000: 388). Identity is elastic, subject to influence from external influences. Identities are shaped by and reflected in communicative texts. Identities are multiple, constructed and reconstructed over time. As Bailey and Hall explain,

> post-structuralist thinking opposes the notion that a person is born with a fixed identity... It suggests instead that identities are floating, that meaning is not fixed and universally true at all times for all people, and that the subject is constructed through the

unconscious in desire, fantasy and memory. Identities are positional in relation to the discourses around us. That is why the notion of representation is so important – identity can only be articulated as a set of representations. Identity is unfixed and... conceptualized as completely and ambiguously caught up within identity processes. (Bailey & Hall, 1992: 20–21)

As we have explored collaborative tourist-destination identity, we have seen that this process applies to the individual – the traveler, the pilgrim – as well as to the community, i.e. the nation, the state, the city, the attraction. And, we have seen that the internet, with its capacity to incorporate a virtual world of information about tourist destinations, plays a seminal role as mediator in this construction process. Franklin explains that for the individual, tourism affords the potential of an identity tied to a place.

Tourism is not only a way of accessing the world, it is increasingly an important means of locating ourselves in it. In a migrant modernity most people are living away from home viewing their home after the manner of tourists; equally among those people and places "left behind" in less migratory flows, tourism often steps in to provide work and a future. As it does so it sifts through people's pasts and, often for the first time, seeks to stamp a cultural identity on the landscape, offering a history to those to whom official history chose to forget. (Franklin, 2003: 26)

Responding to the cooperative interaction of person and place in identity construction, Franklin also explains how the tourist assigns identity to a place.

In visiting the shrines and foundational places of modern nation states the modern tourist performs an affirmation of national identity and citizenship. These types of sites tended to proliferate as nation states became more complex and layered social formations, forever reinventing themselves through wars, exhibitions, anniversaries and other celebrations, heroes and champions, achievements, sporting victories and so on. (Franklin, 2003: 43–44)

Tourism websites are consciously composed to include some texts and exclude others, so that the site constructs for a destination an identity that is both indicative and inviting. Incorporating multiple modalities, website creators exploit patterns and functions of linguistic and visual semiotics. When called up by a potential traveler, the website presents its self as a destination worth exploring, first, electronically on the internet and second, most successfully for the destination, in person. Along the way, because of the collaborative nature of communication, the identity of the destination is negotiated in interaction with the (potential) tourist. In this process, the internet serves as mediator. Complementing this constructivist process for the potential destination, the negotiation nexus contributes to the construction of the tourist's identity as well.

Successful Web and tourist interaction builds community and commonality, thereby contributing to the social construction of both the destination's and tourist's identity. After parenthetically stating 'Today the most cursory tour of the world wide web will furnish dozens of examples, finely differentiated, of official national self-representation', Buzard (2001: 310) continues 'Inserting itself between the increasingly boundary-less tourist market and its own nation's touristic "product," the state implicitly depicted *itself* to the nation as the one agency capable of handling the national autoethnography' (original emphasis). It is the state or its formally structured government tourist board, then, that is responsible for presenting and creating the 'narrative of the nation'. Because they are narrativistic, tourism websites, with their multimodal links to words and to images of localities and people, write and tell stories that position their nations as destinations and their users as tourists. Through these websites, potential tourists are invited to read a story, write a story, co-construct a story as they click, as they view, as they read and as they plan. This story, in turn, becomes a trip-in-waiting – virtual, if not yet actual. Benwell and Stokoe (2006) assert that narratives construct identities. Herman (2007: 308) argues that, on a more cognitive plane, 'narrative functions as a resource for constructing one's own as well as other minds'. Further, Herman (2007: 314) maintains, 'Storytelling practices... themselves help constitute the minds engaged in the production and interpretation of narrative discourse'.

The theoretical models adopted for this analysis lie within the larger framework of discourse analysis. Discourse – defined by van Leeuwen (2005: 94) as 'socially constructed knowledges of (some aspect of) reality... developed in specific social contexts, and in ways which are appropriate to the interests of social actors in these contexts' – is multimodal. The modes that comprise a discourse and through which interpretations of that text are accomplished are interdependent. As Hummon (1988: 201) explains, 'symbolic contrasts are typically implicit, but their existence can be revealed through both textual analysis and the differential use of verbal and visual imagery'. Bowcher writes

What is clear from previous research on multimodality is that although redundancy of meaning may be the result of the simultaneous use of several modes, we cannot say that the resulting meanings that are produced by a multimodal text could be produced if only one mode were to be used. This is because redundancy in meaning does not mean a collection of same meanings just expressed through different modes. (Bowcher, 2007: 242)

A second adopted framework, critical discourse analysis, in seeing discourse as social action, is relevant to this analysis because it contextualizes social problems in texts. As we explore the social action of 'travel and tourism', we view the social 'problem' as what MacCannell (1999: 203) identifies as the desire for a 'locus of a human relationship between un-like-minded individuals, the locus of an urgent desire to share—an intimate connection between one stranger and another, or one generation to another, through the local object' [and] 'a certain kind of human solidarity'. Additionally, we view the 'problem' in the context of the new capitalism as explained by Baranowski and Furlough,

By the mid-twentieth century, nation-states came to see tourism and vacations as essential to the creation of consumer-citizens. Various state, regional, and civic endeavors recognized the value of tourism for the authoritative representation of 'ourselves,' 'our landscape,' and 'our cultural ways and traditions' and in the process forged intimate associations between commerce, community, and collective identities. (Baranowski & Furlough, 2001: 8)

Franklin (2003: 26) concurs, 'Tourism *is* consumerism in a globalizing modernity'.

A third framework, mediated discourse analysis, proves appropriate because of our focus on the role of internet technology in creating communities of practice. Computer-mediated communication offers what Barthes classifies as a 'writerly text' and explains in this way:

here the reader can choose how to relate to the text by negotiating a path through it using different links,..., and networks in a web of info." ...In this ideal text, the networks are many and interact,... this text is a galaxy of signifiers, not a structure of signifieds; it has no beginning; it is reversible; we gain access to it by several entrances. (1978: 44)

Barthes continues,

The writerly text is *ourselves writing*, before the infinite play of the world (the world as function) is traversed, intersected, stopped, plasticized by some singular system (Ideology, Genus, Criticism) which reduces the plurality of entrances, the opening of networks, the infinity of languages.... the networks are many and interact, without any one of them being able to surpass the rest; this text is a galaxy of signifiers, not a structure of signifieds; it has no beginning; it is reversible; we gain access to it by several entrances, none of which can be authoritatively declared to be the main one. (1978: 5)

As potential tourists navigate a tourism web text, they create, out of the links and content they select and the order in which they are selected, a text. This text is reflective of the web text, but it is fully that particular user's created text. It is a text that narrates the destination, but is neither the site creator's narration nor the actual destination itself. Every narrative of a destination is a narrative dialectically produced through interaction between the web user, the web text and the website creator. Every narrative of a destination is also a narrative of the tourist.

The narrative of the destination is akin to a constructed identity for that destination. Enmeshed in the construction and comprehension of the narrative, the reader may find the site and the community it promotes favorable, he/she may find himself/herself acquiring cognitive schema and frames from the experience that come to positively affect his/her view of the world and of him/her self. On the other hand, if the tourist finds the site and the community it promotes dissimilar and unfavorable, he/she may not acquire that same schema and, therefore, experience some measure of cognitive dissonance that leads to a dismissal of the investigated destination as a favorable place to travel. Either no cognitive frame or a cognitive frame that does not fit the tourist's expectations is produced. Tourism website content, then, plays a seminal role in the construction of a 'self' for a destination. When that 'self' is rejected by a potential tourist, the site has failed to capitalize on the community/website/tourist dialectic; the tourist is not constructed as a tourist and the attraction is not constructed for that traveler as a destination.

Our goal with this text has been to inform the reader of the role of the world wide web in mediating the construction of identity. Through the analysis of a number of tourism websites, we have demonstrated how websites, through their use of linguistic and visual texts, serve as mediators of meaning transmission and receipt in the negotiated process of identity construction for the destination presented in the site, the potential tourist and the site itself. Like Hummon, we see

> Tourism, as a social ritual that involves a movement away from the world of home, work, and necessity, [and that] helps define the substance and significance of everyday life by providing an experience of otherness to the traveler. Tourist advertising, as a system of meanings that transforms "ordinary" places into extraordinary tourist worlds, is part of the cultural system that makes this ritual alternation both possible and significant. (Hummon, 1988: 200)

Tourism websites are created for consumers as well as for destinations. They are for initial consumption to encourage further consumption. It is our expectation that this text will similarly be consumed by those who wish to learn more about computer-mediated identity construction. It is our hope that those consumers will be inspired as we are to continue this journey.

For those interested in such a journey, we offer this text as an initial foray into the analysis and understanding of the role of the internet in fostering identity construction for tourists and destinations. This text is an innovation in that it presents the first such analysis that draws on the role of technology in tourism, identity and the new capitalism. Yet, we have just begun; this new medium requires further exploration, especially because of how it may be manipulated and exploited to unconsciously construct narratives of identity. We encourage further analyses of these and other websites that draw on a variety of available frameworks and fields in the social sciences. We particularly encourage analyses that capitalize on the diversity of languages through which tourism identity is constructed. Questions to investigate include whether the visual design theory implied herein is applicable to communities whose writing systems incorporate other than a left-to-right or top-down orientation and whether those websites incorporating a bilingual or multilingual presentation proffer and construct the same identities in the different languages. We wish you well as you embark on your tour.

References

Agar, W. (1996) *Language Shock.* New York: Quill.

Anderson, B.R. (1991) *Imagined Communities: Reflections on the Origin and Spread of Nationalism.* London: Verso.

Aristotle. *Poetics XXII.*

Baider, F., Burger, M. and Goutsos, D. (2005) Introduction. In F. Baider, M. Burger and D. Goutsos (eds) *La Communication Touristique: Approches Discursives de l'Identité et de l'Altérité* [*Tourist Communication: Discursive Approaches to Identity and Otherness*] (pp. 27–43). Paris: L'Harmattan.

Bailey, D.A. and Hall, S. (1992) The vertigo of displacement: Shifts in black documentary practices. *Critical Decade Ten* 8, 14–23.

Baranowski, S. and Furlough, E. (2001) Introduction. In S. Baranowski and E. Furlough (eds) *Being Elsewhere: Tourism, Consumer Culture, and Identity in Modern Europe and North America* (pp. 1–31). Ann Arbor, MI: The University of Michigan Press.

Barthes, R. (1975) *S/Z.* Translated by Richard Miller. New York: Hill and Wang.

Barthes, R. (1978) Rhetoric of the image. In R. Barthes (ed.) *Image, Music, Text* (pp. 32–51) (S. Heath, ed. and trans.). New York: Hill and Wang.

Benwell, B. and Stokoe, E. (2006) *Discourse and Identity.* Edinburgh: Edinburgh University Press.

Bhabha, H.K. (ed.) (1990) *Nation and Narration.* London: Routledge.

Bhattacharya, D. (1997) Mediating India: An analysis of a guidebook. *Annals of Tourism Research* 24, 371–389.

Bowcher, W.L. (2007) A multimodal analysis of good guys and bad guys in Rugby League Week. In T.D. Royce and W.L. Bowcher (eds) *New Directions in the Analysis of Multimodal Discourse* (pp. 239–274). Mahwah, NJ: Lawrence Erlbaum.

Brown, P. (1981) *The Cult of the Saints: Its Rise and Function in Latin Christianity.* Chicago, IL: University of Chicago Press.

Brown, P. and Levinson, S.C. (1987) *Politeness: Some Universals in Language Usage.* Cambridge: Cambridge University Press.

Buzard, J. (1993) *The Beaten Track.* Oxford: Clarendon Press.

Buzard, J. (2001) Culture for export: Tourism and autoethnography in postwar Britain. In S. Baranowski and E. Furlough (eds) *Being Elsewhere: Tourism, Consumer Culture, and Identity in Modern Europe and North America* (pp. 299–319). Ann Arbor, MI: The University of Michigan Press.

Carbaugh, D. (1996) *Situating Selves: The Communication of Social Identities in American Scenes.* New York: SUNY.

Castells, M. (2000) *The Rise of the Network Society.* Oxford: Blackwell.

Chatman, S. (2001) Parody and style. *Poetics Today* 22 (1), 25–39.

Chouliaraki, L. and Fairclough, N. (1999) *Discourse in Late Modernity: Rethinking Critical Discourse Analysis*. Edinburgh: Edinburgh University Press.

Cilauro, S., Gleisner, T. and Sitch, R. (2004a) *Molvanîa: A Land Untouched by Modern Dentistry*. Woodstock, NY: The Overlook Press.

Cilauro, S., Gleisner, T. and Sitch, R. (2004b) *Phaic Tăn: Sunstroke on a Shoestring*. Victoria: Hardie Grant Books.

Cilauro, S., Gleisner, T. and Sitch, R. (2006) *San Sombrero: A Land of Carnivals, Cocktails and Coups*. San Francisco: Chronicle Books.

Ciscel, M.H., Hallett, R.W. and Green, A. (2002) Language attitudes and identity in the European republics of the former Soviet Union. *Texas Linguistic Forum* 44 (1), 48–61.

Cronin, M. (2000) *Across the Lines: Travel, Language, Translation*. Cork: Cork University Press.

Cronin, M. (2006) *Translation and Identity*. London: Routledge.

Crow, M. (2005) *Worst Towns in the U.S.A.* Kingston Upon Thames: TAJ Books.

Dann, G.M.S. (1996) *The Language of Tourism: A Sociolinguistic Perspective*. Wallingford: CAB International.

Diamandaki, K. (2003) Virtual ethnicity and digital diasporas: Identity construction in cyberspace. *Global Media Journal* 2 (2).

Edensor, T. (2002) *National Identity, Popular Culture and Everyday Life*. Oxford and New York: Berg.

Fairclough, N. (1992) *Discourse and Social Change*. London: Polity Press.

Feinstein, H. (1982) Meaning and visual metaphor. *Studies in Art Education* 23 (2), 45–55.

Franklin, A. (2003) *Tourism: An Introduction*. London: Sage.

Friend, T. (2005) The parachute artist: Have Tony Wheeler's guidebooks travelled too far? *The New Yorker* (April 18), 78–91.

Fürsich, E. and Robins, M.B. (2004) Visiting Africa: Constructions of nation and identity on travel websites. *Journal of Asian and African Studies* 39, 133–152.

Gilbert, D. (1999) 'London in all its glory – or how to enjoy London': Guidebook representations of imperial London. *Journal of Historical Geography* 25 (3), 279–297.

Gotham, K.F. (2002) Marketing Mardi Gras: Commodification, spectacle and the political economy of tourism in New Orleans. *Urban Studies* 39 (10), 1735–1756.

Hall, S. (1980) Encoding/ decoding. In S. Hall, D. Hobson, A. Lowe and P. Willis (eds) *Culture, Media and Language* (pp. 128–139). London: Hutchinson.

Hall, S. (1996) The question of cultural identity. In S. Hall, D. Held, D. Hubert and K. Thompson (eds) *Modernity: An Introduction to Modern Societies* (pp. 595–634). Malden, MA: Blackwell.

Hallett, R.W. and Kaplan-Weinger, J. (2004a) The construction of independence: A multimodal discourse analysis of Lithuanian tourism websites. In F. Baider, M. Burger and D. Goutsos (eds) *La Communication Touristique: Approches Discursives de l'identité et de l'altérité/Tourist Communication* [*Discursive Approaches to Identity and Otherness*] (pp. 215–234). Paris: L'Harmattan.

Hallett, R.W. and Kaplan-Weinger, J. (2004b) 'Soup, piece de résistance, entremets and vegetable in one': A critical discourse analysis of Louisiana tourism web sites. Paper presented at the Thirty-third Annual Meeting of the Linguistic Association of the Southwest (LASSO), New Orleans, LA, 10–12 September 2004.

Hallett, R.W. and Kaplan-Weinger, J. (2005) Go or don't go: Balancing promotion and warning in the construction of national identity in travel guides. Paper presented at the Third International Conference on Discourse, Communication, and Enterprise (DICOEN 2005), Rio de Janeiro, Brazil. September 8–10, 2005.

Hallett, R.W. and Kaplan-Weinger, J. (2006) A call to religious festivities: Reconstructing New Orleans tourist by tourist. *Journeys of Expression V.*

Hallett, R.W. and Kaplan-Weinger, J. (2008) 'The place every football fan wants to visit': A discursive analysis of football and soccer halls of fame. In E. Lavric, G. Pisek, A. Skinner and W. Stadler (eds) *The Linguistics of Football* (pp. 211–220). Tübingen: Gunter Narr.

Hannam, K. and Knox, D. (2005) Discourse analysis in tourism research: A critique. *Tourism Recreation Research* 30 (2), 23–30.

Harré, R. and van Langehove, L. (1999) Reflexive positioning: Autobiography. In R. Harré and L. van Langehove (eds) *Positioning Theory: Moral Contexts of Intentional Actions* (pp. 60–73). Oxford: Blackwell.

Henderson, J.C. (2003) The politics of tourism in Myanmar. *Current Issues in Tourism* 6 (2), 97–118.

Herman, D. (2007) Storytelling and the sciences of mind: Cognitive narratology, discursive psychology, and narratives in face-to-face interaction. *Narrative* 15 (3), 306–334.

Howard, J.A. (2000) Social psychology of identities. *Annual Review of Sociology* 26, 367–393.

Hummon, D.M. (1988) Tourist worlds: Tourist advertising, ritual, and American culture. *The Sociological Quarterly* 29, 179–202.

Hutcheon, L. (1989) *The Politics of Postmodernism*. London: Routledge.

Jack, G. and Phipps, A. (2005) *Tourism and Intercultural Exchange: Why Tourism Matters*. Clevedon: Channel View Publications.

Jaworski, A. and Pritchard, A. (eds) (2005) *Discourse, Communication and Tourism*. Clevedon: Channel View Publications.

Jaworski, A. and Thurlow, C. (2004) Language, tourism and globalization: Mapping new international identities. In S.H. Ng, C.N. Candlin and C.Y. Chiu (eds) *Language Matters: Communication, Identity, and Culture* (pp. 291–321). Hong Kong: City University of Hong Kong Press.

Johnstone, B. (2002) *Discourse Analysis*. Oxford: Blackwell.

Kaufman, S.K. (2001) Selling Lourdes: Pilgrimage, tourism, and the mass-marketing of the sacred in nineteenth-century France. In S. Baranowski and E. Furlough (eds) *Being Elsewhere: Tourism, Consumer Culture, and Identity in Modern Europe and North America* (pp. 63–88). Ann Arbor, MI: The University of Michigan Press.

Kövecses, Z. (2002) *Metaphor: A Practical Introduction*. New York: Oxford.

Kress, G. and van Leeuwen, T. (1996) *Reading Images: The Grammar of Visual Design*. London: Routledge.

Kress, G. and van Leeuwen, T. (1998) Front pages: (The critical) analysis of newspaper layout. In A. Bell and P. Garrett (eds) *Approaches to Media Discourse* (pp. 186–219). Oxford: Blackwell.

Kress, G. and van Leeuwen, T. (2001) *Multimodal Discourse: The Modes and Media of Contemporary Communication*. London: Arnold.

Laderman, S. (2002) Shaping memory of the past: Discourse in travel guidebooks for Vietnam. *Mass Communication and Society* 3 (1), 87–110.

Lakoff, G. and Johnson, M. (1980) *Metaphors We Live By*. Chicago, IL: University of Chicago Press.

Lane, J.B. (ed.) (2006) *Steel Shavings: Gary's First Hundred Years: A Centennial History of Gary, Indiana, 1906–2006* (Vol. 37). Valparaiso, IN: Home Mountain.

Larkin, E. (2005) *Finding George Orwell in Burma*. New York: Penguin Press.

Le, E. (2006) *The Spiral of Anti-Other Rhetoric: Discourses of Identity and the International Media Echo*. Amsterdam: John Benjamins.

Leborg, C. (2006) *Visual Grammar*. New York: Princeton Architectural Press.

Liestøl, G. (1994) Wittgenstein, Genette, and the reader's narrative in hypertext. In G.P. Landow (ed.) *Hyper/Text/Theory* (pp. 87–120). Baltimore, MD: The Johns Hopkins University Press.

Link, M. (2005) World books. *Real Simple* (June), 185–189.

Locke, T. (2004) *Critical Discourse Analysis*. London: Continuum.

MacCannell, D. (1999) *The Tourist: A New Theory of the Leisure Class*. Berkeley, CA: University of California Press.

Mahon, J.E. (1999) Getting your sources right: What Aristotle *didn't* say. In L. Cameron and G. Low (eds) *Researching and Applying Metaphor* (pp. 69–80). Cambridge: Cambridge University Press.

Martin, S., Looby, M., Clark, M. and Cummings, J. (2002) *Lonely Planet Myanmar (Burma)* (8th edn). Melbourne: Lonely Planet Publications.

Matthiessan, C.M.I.M. (2007) The multimodal page: A systemic functional exploration. In T.D. Royce and W.L. Bowcher (eds) *New Directions in the Analysis of Multimodal Discourse* (pp. 1–62). Mahwah, NJ: Lawrence Erlbaum.

Mead, G.H. (1934) *Mind, Self and Society*. Chicago, IL: University of Chicago Press.

Mitra, A. (1997) Virtual commonality: Looking for India on the Internet. In S. Jones (ed.) *Virtual Culture: Identity and Communication in Cybersociety* (pp. 55–79). Thousand Oaks, CA: Sage.

Morley, D. and Robins, K. (1995) *Spaces of Identity: Global Media, Electronic Landscapes and Cultural Boundaries*. New York: Routledge.

Nilsen, A.P. and Nilsen, D.L.F. (2000) *Encyclopedia of 20th-Century American Humor*. Westport, CT: Oryx Press.

Nolan, M.L. and Nolan, S. (1989) *Christian Pilgrimage in Modern Western Europe*. Chapel Hill, NC: University of North Carolina Press.

Phipps, A. (2007) *Learning the Arts of Linguistic Survival: Languaging, Tourism, Life*. Clevedon: Channel View.

Porter, D. and Prince, D. (2001) *Frommer's Spain 2001*. Indianapolis, IN: IDG Books Worldwide.

Pritchard, A. and Morgan, N. (2005) Representations of 'ethnographic knowledge': Early comic postcards of Wales. In A. Jaworski and A. Pritchard (eds) *Discourse, Communication and Tourism* (pp. 53–75). Clevedon: Channel View Publications.

Raskin, V. (1985) *Semantic Mechanisms of Humor*. Dordrecht: D. Reidel.

Ritzer, G. and Liska, A. (1997) 'McDisneyization' and 'post-tourism': Contemporary perspectives on contemporary tourism. In C. Rojek and J. Urry (eds) *Touring Cultures: Transformations of Travel and Theory* (pp. 96–109). London: Routledge.

Robinson, M. and Smith, M. (2006) Politics, power and play: The shifting contexts of cultural tourism. In M. Smith and M. Robinson (eds) *Cultural Tourism in a Changing World: Politics, Participation and (Re)Presentation* (pp. 1–17). Clevedon: Channel View Publications.

Roche, M. (2000) *Mega-events and Modernity*. London: Routledge.

Rojek, C. and Urry, J. (1997) Transformations of travel and theory. In C. Rojek and J. Urry (eds) *Touring Cultures: Transformations of Travel and Theory* (pp. 1–19). London: Routledge.

Royce, T.D. (2007) Intersemiotic complementarity: A framework for multimodal discourse analysis. In T.D. Royce and W.L. Bowcher (eds) *New Directions in the Analysis of Multimodal Discourse* (pp. 63–109). Mahwah, NJ: Lawrence Erlbaum.

Rudolph, C. (2004) *Pilgrimage to the End of the World: The Road to Santiago de Compostela*. Chicago, IL: University of Chicago Press.

Schiffrin, D. (2004) Discourse analysis and conversation analysis/Diskurs und Konversationsanalyse. In U. Ammon, N. Dittmar, K.J. Mattheiser and P. Trudgill (eds) *Sociolinguistics/Soziolinguistik: Ein Internationales Handbuch zur Wissenschaft von Sprache und Gesellschaft [An International Handbook of the Science of Language and Society]* (pp. 88–98). New York: de Gruyter.

Schmitt, R.I. and Leonard, W.M. II (1986) Immortalizing the self through sport. *The American Journal of Sociology* 91 (5), 1088–1111.

Schneider, S.M. and Foot, K.A. (2004) The web as an object of study. *New Media and Society* 6 (1), 114–122.

Schultz, P. (2003) *1,000 Places to See Before You Die*. New York: Workman Publishing Company.

Scollon, R. (2001) *Mediated Discourse: The Nexus of Practice*. London: Routledge.

Stiglitz (n.d.) On WWW at http://nobelprize.org/nobel_prizes/economics/laureates/2001/stiglitz-autobio.html.

Tannen, D. (2007) *Talking Voices: Repitition, Dialogue, and Imagery in Conversational Discourse*. Cambridge: Cambridge University Press.

Traubel, H. (1906) *With Walt Whitman in Camden*, Vol. IV. On WWW at www.whitmanarchive.org/criticism/disciples/traubel/WWWiC/4/med.00004.77.html.

Turner, V. and Turner, E. (1978) *Image and Pilgrimage in Christian Culture: Anthropological Perspectives*. New York: Columbia University Press.

Urry, J. (1995) *Consuming Places*. London: Routledge.

Urry, J. (2002) *The Tourist Gaze* (2nd edition). London: Sage.

van Leeuwen, T. (2005) *Introducing Social Semiotics*. New York: Routledge.

van Leeuwen, T. and Jewitt, C. (2001) *Handbook of Visual Analysis*. London: Sage.

Washington, R.E. and Karen, D. (2001) Sport and society. *Annual Review of Sociology* 27, 187–212.

Wodak, R., de Cillia, R., Reisigl, M. and Leibhart, K. (1999) *The Discursive Construction of National Identity* (A. Hirsch and R. Mitten, trans.). Edinburgh: Edinburgh University Press.

Wright, S. (2000) *Community and Communication: The Role of Language in Nation State Building and European Integration*. Clevedon: Multilingual Matters.

Young, T.R. (1986) The sociology of sport: Structural Marxist and cultural Marxist approaches. *Sociological Perspectives* 29 (1), 3–28.

Index

Subject index

baseball xiii, 57, 61, 62, 64, 65, 69-81
basketball 57, 61-63, 65, 66, 69-71, 74-75, 77, 81-84, 86

discourse analysis 6-8, 10-13, 15-16, 19, 23, 32-33, 35, 39, 45, 57, 91, 115-116, 118, 119
– critical discourse analysis 6, 7-8, 10, 15, 33, 57, 115, 116, 119
– mediated discourse analysis 6, 8, 11, 19
– multimodal (discourse) analysis 6, 7, 10-12, 13, 15, 16, 23, 32, 35, 39, 45, 57, 91, 118, 119

English language 1, 3, 4, 17, 89

globalization 8
guidebooks 2, 4, 87, 89, 114

halls of fame 4, 69-86
Hurricane Katrina 44, 45, 48, 51, 52, 53, 54, 55
hypertext 8, 10, 16, 35, 39, 68

identity xv, xvi, 4, 5, 6-14, 15-19, 21, 23, 25, 28, 31, 32, 33, 35, 39-40, 42-43, 44-46, 48, 51, 53, 55, 57-59, 61, 65, 68, 71, 73, 77-78, 86, 87, 89, 91, 102-103, 114-118, 120, 121
– construction of identity 5, 6, 9-11, 14, 15-16, 18, 32, 35, 39-40, 46, 57, 114, 117, 120-121
– formation of identity 8, 11, 23, 68
– national identity 6, 7, 15-16, 18-19, 21, 23, 87, 103, 116-117
– tourist identity 8, 13, 118

linguistic relativism 13
localization 10, 34
Lonely Planet 2, 87-89, 97, 99-100, 107

Mardi Gras 44, 53-55

metaphor 5, 12-13, 29, 37, 39-40, 45-46, 48-52, 55-56, 57-63, 67-68, 72, 75, 82, 98, 100, 116

nationalism 9, 69-86, 116
new capitalism 2, 9, 15, 61, 91, 95, 100, 119, 121

parody 101-113, 116
pilgrims/pilgrimage xiv, 5, 8, 10, 33-43, 44-45, 53, 68, 69, 71, 77, 81, 83-86, 116-117

Self/Other 5, 6, 10, 15, 19, 21, 22, 26, 29, 36, 45, 53, 57, 70-71, 88, 94, 101, 102, 103, 104, 106, 107, 113, 114, 115, 118, 120, 121
semiotics 11-12, 42, 92, 117
– semiotic analysis 11, 83
– social semiotics 11
– visual semiotics 10, 11, 23, 24, 28, 29, 39, 40, 42, 44, 46, 57, 83, 92, 116, 117
soccer 69, 71, 77
social action 2, 6, 7, 10, 12, 15, 16, 32, 33, 45, 53, 54, 57, 95, 96, 99, 115, 116, 119
social construction/constructionism xvi, 6, 7, 8, 11, 16-18, 23, 42, 70, 71, 75, 115, 116, 118

tourism xi, xiii-vxi, 1-5, 6-9, 11-14, 15-21, 23-25, 28-29, 31, 33, 35, 37-38, 42-43, 44-45, 48- 49, 51-55, 59, 61, 68, 69, 71, 86, 87-91, 93-98, 100, 101-104, 114-121
– collage tourism 3
– discourse of xi, 1, 2, 3, 5, 14, 100
translation 4, 22, 104

visual design theory 8, 11, 23, 40, 48, 85, 91, 97, 121

World Wide Web xiv-xv, 1, 3, 6-8, 10, 15, 68, 114, 118, 120

Place index

Author index